Twayne's English Authors Series

EDITOR OF THIS VOLUME

Sylvia E. Bowman
Indiana University

James Harrington

TEAS 188

James Harrington

*from a portrait attributed to A. Van der Venne in the
National Portrait Gallery, London*

JAMES HARRINGTON

By MICHAEL DOWNS
Indiana University at Fort Wayne

TWAYNE PUBLISHERS
A DIVISION OF G. K. HALL & CO., BOSTON

Library of Congress Cataloging in Publication Data

Downs, Michael.
  James Harrington.

  (Twayne's English authors series ; TEAS 188)
  Bibliography: p. 145 - 47
  Includes index.
  1.   Harrington, James, 1611 - 1677.
JC153.H4D68   320.5'092'4   77-21418
ISBN 0-8057-6693-6

Contents

About the Author

Michael Clark Downs is associate professor of Political Science at Indiana University-Purdue University at Fort Wayne. He received his A.B. from Aquinas College and his A.M. and Ph.D. from the University of Notre Dame. In addition to a Woodrow Wilson Fellowship, Downs has received a National Defense Education Act Fellowship, a Notre Dame Dissertation Fellowship and an Indiana University Faculty Fellowship. His major research efforts have been directed toward an understanding of the concepts of property and family in the tradition of English political theory.

In addition to his teaching Downs is active in the political life of the Fort Wayne community and presently serves as a member of the local election board and the board of election canvassers. These are posts in which his appreciation for James Harrington's intricate electoral procedures has sharpened. These experiences have also served as a basis for a series of studies of local politics.

Downs holds memberships in all of the major professional associations and is an active participant in faculty governance at Indiana University.

Preface

Some writers demand our attention; others deserve it. The landscape of American politics—practice, constitution, theoretical justification, and even its study—is arranged according to a plan devised by James Harrington in the seventeenth century. If this landscape isn't pleasing, if its prospects are not always pleasant, it is still a functional, though quaint, design. Planned and assembled to endure, it has confirmed James Harrington's expectations. But for reasons easily explained, Harrington does not demand the attention of scholars and students. That attention is the portion of John Locke and Charles L. de Secondat de Montesquieu, the other two members of the trinity cited in American government textbooks as responsible for the theoretical origins of our political system. Locke's *Second Treatise on Government* and Montesquieu's *L'Esprit des lois* are clearly broader and deeper than anything Harrington wrote.

Harrington's great misfortune is that his most profound observations about the first causes of politics are embedded in the extremely unwieldy *Commonwealth of Oceana*, a work that requires considerable assiduity from its readers. His liveliest prose is found in the pamphlets he fired off in the numerous controversies that were sparked by the publication of *Oceana* and by the feverish politics that came between the death of Oliver Cromwell and the return of the Stuarts. These publications were occasional pieces best understood in reference to the minutiae of day-to-day events and obscure theological disputes. To write in a sprightly way about small things and flatly about great things is not a charge laid by critics against Locke and Montesquieu.

Moreover, Locke and Montesquieu were also fortunate either in their purpose for writing or in the times in which they wrote. Locke wrote, in part at least, to justify a state of affairs in England that settled a serious problem and confirmed popular prejudice; and Montesquieu had nothing to fear from his king. Harrington, on the other hand, proposed what very few wanted and found himself at cross purposes with the clergy, his own class, and finally with the king. He suffered criticism, scorn, and imprisonment for his profession; and the value placed on his work faded in his own lifetime when his weakened mind and body failed him.

In addition to the interest that might be generated by the often cited but seldom studied influence of James Harrington on American politics, he was also an interesting man who lived an unusually fascinating life. At a time in English history when public life was filled with arresting personalities, Harrington held his own. He was known by kings and regicides; by poets, soldiers, scholars, politicians; by Presbyterians and Episcopalians, by Monarchists and Republicans. During the protracted trial and imprisonment of Charles I and again while Parliament debated the Commonwealth out of existence, he was present—center stage—and, though he was unable either to make peace or to realize his plan for an English Republic, even his failures are worth considering.

Caught up in controversy with the proponents of different solutions to England's political problems during his public career, Harrington has been a factor in the scholarly battle among modern social historians over the role played by the gentry in the English Civil War and in the Restoration. R. H. Tawney, H. R. Trevor-Roper, and J. H. Hexter are only the most prominent combatants in this encounter that now stretches over several academic generations. The dust still has not settled.

Harrington believed that he had discovered an important political truth. Machiavelli and Aristotle may have been aware, before Harrington, of a strong affinity between property and power; but it was Harrington who stated the principle bluntly and unequivocably: since people need to eat to live, whoever—be it one, few, or many—controls the land that produces the food possesses the power to rule. When Harrington explained the civil war and proposed the remedy for England's malady, both event and solution were based on applications of his discovery about food, land, and power. Whether his analysis was correct is the point in question among social and economic historians, but the degree to which he spoke for the land-owning gentry as a class is also in doubt.

Political scientists, particularly those who are interested in placing their discipline upon a firm empirical footing, may be interested in the efforts of an earlier generation to do so. Living and studying at a time when an old order was crumbling, Harrington said with clarity that politics would become deliverance if ambiguity could be replaced with certainty. He tried, not very systematically it must be observed, to create that certainty by invoking the shade of William

Harvey, the anatomist, to lend the method used in *Oceana* some authority; and he employed the terminology of the new sciences in his writing. Though he may not always have been accurate, he relied upon observation and historical case studies to a degree remarkable at the time. The modern fields of comparative government and interest group analysis within the discipline of political science may owe as much to Harrington as the United States Constitution does. For the *Commonwealth of Oceana* reviews and evaluates no fewer than eleven constitutions; and Harrington's analysis of English politics adopts an interest group approach that views political groups as creatures controlled and produced by economic forces.

This study deals with the aspects of James Harrington's life, career, theories, and the influence mentioned above. The first chapter considers Harrington's great discovery, the principle of the balance between property and power. Harrington's early life, viewed in relation to the principle of balance, is the subject of the second chapter. The third chapter is concerned with the nature of commonwealths and of the equal commonwealth—the species of that form of government that Harrington believed to be best. The place of the social sciences, history, economics, and political science in his work and the use Harrington made of empirical data are discussed in Chapter 4. The last chapter describes the specific proposals that Harrington made for England in the *Oceana;* their effect and reception in England at the time they were written; and the influence that Harrington subsequently had in France, England, and America. The summary and conclusions of this study, included in the last chapter, will return the reader to the point of beginning, the point of this preface, that James Harrington is a writer and theorist who deserves attention.

A note about Harrington sources is appropriate. He wrote intensively for five years, explaining and defending his ideas and plans. A translation of books iii and iv of Virgil's *Aeneid,* published by him during this period, gives evidence that he was able to enlist another muse in his campaign to popularize the *Commonwealth of Oceana* and his theory of balance. This translation, an essay upon two of Virgil's *Eclogues, Oceana,* and twenty other works of various lengths are the entire corpus of his published work. Except for the translation and the essay, all are found in the 1771 edition of *James Harrington Works.* This edition, compiled by John Toland in 1699, and later expanded by others to include the pamphlets, is the one most available through reprints 'to scholars and the general public and is cited in this book. References to the *Commonwealth of Oceana* also cite the scholarly edition of that work painstakingly researched by Sven B. Liljegren and published in 1924. His effort is a major contribution to Harrington scholarship and is indispensable to serious students. It is, unfortunately, no longer in print.

I am grateful to Indiana University at Fort Wayne for the support given my research; the library staff of this institution has been patient and helpful; the administration has assisted me by providing time in which to study and reflect; my colleagues, especially in the Political Science Department, are always a source of ideas and intellectual stimulation; and my students, who have been listening to much of what appears in this book for some time now, have, I hope, forgiven me much. In addition, the Indiana University Foundation awarded me a Summer Research Fellowship that was invaluable during the early stages of my work.

Two friends, Barbara Blauvelt and Jeanette Reitz, deserve more praise and thanks than words can bear. Their attention to the detail I tend to overlook and their efficiency at reproducing what I so inefficiently produce have been indispensable. My wife, Mary, and our children, so tolerant of scholarly obsession, are due much credit; for they make our home an excellent place in which to write and live.

MICHAEL DOWNS

Fort Wayne, Indiana

Chronology

1603   The first member of the House of Stuart, James VI of Scotland, becomes King James I of England; the Millenary Petition is presented to him.

1605   The Gunpowder Plot.

1611   James Harrington born in Northamptonshire on January 3; King James Bible published; Sir Edward Coke becomes chief justice and begins his opposition to the crown.

1618   Thirty Years' War begins.

1620   Sir Francis Bacon publishes *Novum Organum;* establishment of Plymouth Plantation in North America.

1621   Impeachment and fall of Bacon from power.

1622   Parliament dissolved after asserting its prerogative to speak freely on foreign affairs.

1625   Charles I succeeds James as king.

1626   Impeachment of Charles' favorite, the Duke of Buckingham; publication of *The New Atlantis* by Frances Bacon.

1628   Parliament passes the Petition of Right; Buckingham assassinated.

1629   Harrington enters Trinity College, Oxford; Charles I rules without Parliament until 1640.

1631   Harrington leaves the university after his father's death; travels in Europe until 1635.

c.1637 Charles I appoints Harrington a gentleman of the privy chamber extraordinary.

1639   Harrington accompanies Charles I to Scotland during the Bishops' War.

1640   The Long Parliament commences; sits until 1660.

1642   The First Civil War begins.

1644 -   Harrington active on behalf of the elector of Palatine with
1645   Parliament.

1646   First Civil War ends.

1647   Harrington joins Charles I in confinement, then travels with him to the Isle of Wight; Parliament appoints him groom of the bedchamber.

1648   Second Civil War breaks out.

1649   Charles I executed; Harrington retires to his estates.

1651   Thomas Hobbes' *Leviathan* published.

1653   Oliver Cromwell becomes lord protector; Instrument of Government adopted.

1656   *The Commonwealth of Oceana* published, in part as an answer to Hobbes' *Leviathan; Pian Piano* published.

1658   *Prerogative of Popular Government, Oceana* (second edition), translations of books iii and iv of Virgil's *Aeniad, Seven Models of a Commonwealth* all published; Cromwell dies.

1659   The Rota Club founded; *Pour enclouer le canon; A Discourse upon this saying. . . ; The Art of Lawgiving; A Discourse shewing. . . ; Politicastor; Political Aphorisms; A Parallel of the Spirit of the People;* and *Valerius and Publicola* all published; Harringtonians petition Parliament to consider establishing a commonwealth.

1660   The Rota Club dissolves; *The Ways and Means. . . , The Rota* both published; The House of Stuart restored; Charles II becomes king.

1661   Harrington writes *System of Politics;* arrested and imprisoned.

1662   Imprisonment continues; harsh treatment results in ill health, mental instability; Harrington released; his last years spent in retirement.

1675   Harrington marries his childhood sweetheart, the daughter of Sir Marmaduke Dorrell.

1677   After a long illness, Harrington dies.

CHAPTER 1

Property and Power

D URING the early summer in England, 1962, graduate student Felix Raab was working on a study of Machiavelli's influence on seventeenth and eighteenth century English political thought when he confronted a problem that still presents a challenge to all who study the writings of James Harrington. In preparing notes for a chapter, "Harrington, Hobbes, God and Machiavelli," which now appears in *The English Face of Machiavelli*, Raab discovered fourteen different James Harringtons—fourteen distinctly different interpretations of his theories. Since then several more James Harringtons have been added to Raab's list.[1]

This phenomenon is not uncommon. Many who have developed theories about politics have suffered this fate; and we may ask, at the beginning of a book that may encourage the additional proliferation of Harringtons, why this happens. Charles Blitzer, the author of the most thorough study of Harrington, thought at first that "this variety of interpretations may in itself suggest something of the richness of Harrington's thought." But Blitzer realized, as he explained his own point of view and method, that much of the variety might be traced to disarray among scholars with different viewpoints and different methods who undertake to explain Harrington to us.[2] This second possibility was persuasively argued by Judith Shklar, whose evaluation of Harrington—"provocative minor writer"—certainly denies, rather than suggests, that Blitzer's tentative first answer—that Harrington's richness lay at the heart of all the argument about him—was the correct one. Professor Shklar thought that Harrington's theories were obscured by "the intrusion of ideology upon historical analysis" that occurs in three ways: the desire of later writers to see in Harrington their own political preferences and ideas, a desire usually all too persuasive; the use made of individual theorists by some historians to endow abstract

13

terms such as "bourgeois" and "feudal" with reality; and the technique of treating individual theorists as the product or representative of some social whole.[3]

The existence of fourteen Harringtons so impressed Felix Raab that he included a brief description of each. While some accepted Harrington's theory of social change and believed it correct, others believed him to be a Utopian dreamer; but,

From another point of view, he could be seen as a primative forerunner of Karl Marx, or, alternatively, as the misguided apologist / prophet of the bourgeois revolution. On the other hand, it was possible to deny the element of determinism in his analysis, and to place "the Empire of Law" at the centre of his thought.

More generally, he could be seen as a man of the Renaissance, a "humanistisch erzogener Politiker," and as a Hobbesian mechanist, corrected by the empiricism of Machiavelli. To one author he was yet one more exponent of the mixed state, to another, "*Oceana* is a Machiavellian meditation upon feudalism," to a third he appeared as a scientist, the Harvey of politics. He can look like a typical Independent, and he can lend weight to the neo-Hegelian racism which was fashionable in German historiography of the nineteen-thirties.[4]

And Raab concludes by adding Professor Shklar's own Harrington, an early "re-statement of the 'survivalist tradition'," to his list.

Because Raab's own work had a different purpose, he made no effort to evaluate these interpretations. He merely observed that most of them had "some contact with the reality of Harrington's thought" but that they had depended upon "presuppositions about the period . . . which have little connection with Harrington." The need for a synthesis to bring some order to this scholarly confusion was obvious. But the synthesis had to be based upon a careful and direct reference to the texts, a method complying with Professor Shklar's admonition: "Anyone who wishes to know exactly what Harrington said must read him."[5]

But just reading Harrington would not be sufficient for understanding what he meant. There would, perhaps, be only one James Harrington left, but this remaining Harrington would be a pallid thinker, and he would not be of much assistance in understanding the place of his ideas and experience in our tradition. "It is, indeed, the mere cataloguing of 'who said what' that has brought the study of the history of ideas to its present low repute," said Shklar. Although Raab was correct in asserting that commentators have spent more time elaborating a context that is not relevant, he has not granted anyone a license to ignore the seventeenth century in England when reading Harrington's *The Commonwealth of Oceana*, his *Art of Lawgiving*, or even Hobbes' *Leviathan*.

Few of the scholars who have produced interpretations of Harrington's theories wrote with the avowed intention of understanding him; most have been more interested in using him, not always for ideological motives, to flesh out their own arguments about an age, class, or movement—by turning to him for support rather than for light. Few entire monographs have been allocated to Harrington, his works, and his theories. In longer works in which Harrington appears, he seems to enter and to exit like an underdeveloped two dimensional character acting in a stock role. In other words, earlier treatments of Harrington are unsatisfactory because they lack an appreciation of the problem contained in the statement that every text has a context. Slighting one or the other produces distortion as surely as any ideological preconception. Finding the unity, or the lack of it, between text and context is the task set for us by any writer; for every flight of fancy must begin somewhere and at some time.

Thinking about politics is a restless preoccupation; the thinker moves back and forth among different aspects and settings, from the most mundane and even sordid varieties of activity to the most sublime. The language of politics is spoken in the precinct, the university, and even in the church; the existence of this language may be taken as evidence that thinking about politics is taking place, though it may prove that the quality of the thinking is not very high.

Political hacks and statesmen, political scientists, political philosophers and theorists, and theologians look to one another as well as within themselves for the resolution of a problem, the verification of a theory, justification for an act, or a means of deliverance. Michael Oakeshott, writing about Thomas Hobbes, a more famous contemporary of Harrington's, observed that "Probably there has been no theory of the nature of the world, of the activity of man, of the destiny of mankind, no theology or cosmology, perhaps even no metaphysics, that has not sought a reflection of itself in the mirror of political philosphy; certain there has been no fully considered politics that has not looked for its reflection in eternity"[6]—nor, perhaps, any fully considered political act. Whether this reflection is sought consciously or by instinct, it is an attempt to find unity or harmony in the universe of man, society, the state, and nature.

When, for example, someone says, "Winning isn't everything," the speaker is perhaps appalled at what is being done to win. "But not winning is absolutely nothing" is the view of one who is annoyed at the suggestion of wrongdoing or, at best, at the proposal of an enervating restraint. In both statements, the speakers are expressing reactions to the problem of unity. In this case, the speakers want unity on their own terms—a unity that is probably impossible in a world where both continue to insist on pursuing competing and incompatible ends. Indeed, the unity may be impossible on any terms; for a proposal for unity that would abolish the precinct, the university, or the church will satisfy only those who want, or already see, a simpler world. The unity traditionally sought, the unity that integrates them all, has never been found. This search is the challenge that confronts, on different levels, the politician, the political scientist and theorist, and the political philosopher.

I   *The Balance in Harrington's Works*

James Harrington addressed the problem of unity under exciting and trying circumstances. His response to it, the methods he developed to deal with it, and the success and failure he experienced applying his method in analysis and in action are an interesting part of the history of political thinking and acting.

It is appropriate, therefore, for us to begin with Harrington's major text, *The Commonwealth of Oceana*, and with its primary context, the life and experience of the man who wrote it. The *Oceana*, Harrington's first work on politics, is his first elaboration of the theory upon which his reputation is based. That power is determined by the distribution of property—the principle of the balance—is the basis of the originality claimed for Harrington by himself and others. As John Toland, his first editor and second biographer, wrote in the introduction to Harrington's *Works*, "That empire follows the balance of property, whether lodg'd in one, in a few, or in many hands, he was the first that ever made out; and [it] is a noble discovery, where of the honor solely belongs to him, as much as those of the circulation of the blood, of printing, of guns, of the compass, or of optic glasses, to the several authors."[7]

This is an early evaluation of the balance; and, in paying tribute to the nobility and originality of its discovery, Toland indirectly pays it the highest compliment that a seventeenth or eighteenth century intellectual can bestow: the balance is a discovery that is useful in the way that optic glasses are; is as scientific and useful as the discovery of the circulation of the blood; and is beneficial to mankind. On one occasion, Harrington was more modest about his contribution. When one of his contemporary critics accused him of claiming credit for a discovery that was really Aristotle's, he replied, "If the Considerer thinks that I have strain'd courtesy with Aristotle . . . further than is warrantable, in relation to the balance, be it as he pleases; I who must either have the more of Authority, or the less of Competition shall lose neither way."[8] On other occasions, Harrington was less modest and more vociferous in rejecting claims put forward on behalf of other authors.

Instead of any of the Harringtons created by scholars, the original Harrington would have preferred to be recognized as the man who discovered the balance.

Harrington's balance states that changes in the distribution of property are the changes in history; the concentration of ownership, or its decentralization, is the key to an analysis of any society; if the balance is awry, it may be the cause of civil war; if properly stabilized, the balance is the basis of an immortal commonwealth. Like the dialectic with other theorists, the balance is indispensable to Harrington's efforts to construct a unified and harmonious political universe.

II   *The Balance*

"To begin with riches, in regard that men are hung upon these, not of choice but of necessity and by the teeth: for as much as he who wants bread, is his servant that will feed him; if a man feeds a whole people, they are under his empire."[9] This statement, blunt and somewhat awkwardly put, appears in "Preliminaries I" of *Oceana* and defines a stark reality: there are two great classes of people, those without bread, or much else either, and those who have enough for themselves and others too. Here, with all pretense aside, is the relationship between these peoples: dependence and necessity on one side; dominion and empire on the other. All people, he will say in another place, are either free men or servants. The free men can live of themselves; the servants cannot.[10]

This view presents the balance in its most basic form. Not only is it written without any attempt to soften its impact, but it also begins with the simplest human relationship—individual to individual. It is "he," one person, who wants bread and who becomes "his" servant. From an observation made in a micropolitical setting, Harrington enlarged his field to include an "empire," for he held that his principle also governs families: "Where the eldest of many brothers has all, or so much that the rest of their livelihood stand in need of him, that brother is as it were a prince in that family." The balance is, therefore, a principle that is universal in its application in societies, from primary to secondary, from local to national, and even, we will see, from national to international.

Harrington in discussing and elaborating the balance uses three terms: riches, wealth, and property. In the case of each term, however, the real constituents of power are land, money, or goods. Though empire, dominion, or power depends on some mix of these three, land, money, and goods are really no more than the raw material that support the true instrument of power—an army. If an empire depends on physical force, the ability to command military power is paramount. The two kinds of empire, domestic or foreign, depend for their definition upon the nationality and geographic situation of the subjects as well as upon the methods used to maintain them. Domestic empire is established according to the distribution of property—according to the number of people who own or control a preponderance of the *landed* property. This preponderance is set at "three parts in four." If one man controls this preponderance, "his empire is an absolute monarchy"; if a few men exert this control, Harrington called it a "mixed monarchy"; and, if the whole people are more or less equal landlords, the empire may be termed a "commonwealth."[11]

This classification, or typology, of governments has ancient origins. The criterion is empirical; the state will be governed by one, few, or many. Aristotle had used it in *The Politics*; and in Harrington's own time, Hobbes had relied upon it in the *Leviathan*. Since Aristotle and Harrington added normative elements to the list considered in classifying governments, this criteria enabled them to distinguish between good and bad forms. Aristotle linked concepts that developed from each level of political activity, from the practical world to the sublime. In his typology, good rulers, one, few, or many, were motivated by an unselfish regard for the entire community: "Whenever the One, the Few, or the Many rule with a view to the commonweal, these constitutions must be right; but if they look to the advantage of one section only, be it the One the Few or the Mass, it is a deviation."[12]

The good forms are called kingship, aristocracy, and polity; the corresponding bad forms are tyranny, oligarchy, and democracy. In good forms, the commonweal is protected by the rule of law—a formulation of reason in harmony both with the community and the divine—and a governing class is composed of men who are able to live what Aristotle called "the good life." These men had personal fortunes that freed them from want and work and made it possible for them to unite a life of action in politics with thought and reflection. The best governments, however, were always prey to the ravages of change; and Aristotle, essentially conservative, placed a high value on stability and permanence. Among good forms, he established another ranking, based upon his evaluation of the relative stability of each form. Polities, in his studies, had greater potential for both adaptability and stability and were superior for that reason to kingships and aristocracies. Theoretically, at least, this typology pays respect to each aspect of the political universe, from physical nature to metaphysics. Aristotle's is an early effort to establish that desired unity, and its authority in Medieval Europe was unchallenged. In seventeenth century England, its authority was attacked directly by some thinkers and undermined by others.

When Thomas Hobbes attacked it, he particularly attacked its normative criteria. The empirical classification of governments into those in which one, few, or many exercised the sovereign power was valid; but the division of forms of government into good and bad was only a matter of individual preference: "There be other names of government, in the histories and books of policy; as tyranny, and oligarchy: but they are not the names of other forms of government, but of the same forms misliked. For they that are discontented under monarchy, call it tyranny; and they that are displeased with aristocracy, call it oligarchy: so also, they which find themselves grieved under a democracy, call it anarchy, which signifies want of government . . ."[13] Hobbes denies the existence of any objective standard that, if applied to forms of government, could distinguish those that are good from those that are not. He responded to an urge or experience that contradicts both Aristotle and the Medieval Scholasticism that grew out of the Aristotelian view of the world.

James Harrington must be listed among those thinkers who began by affirming much of what Aristotle said but ended by subtly altering it. This alteration, undertaken sincerely and for the purpose of perfecting what Aristotle was perceived to have left unfinished, failed to fulfill its promise. From its place of authority, Aristotelian political thought was reduced to a point where it was merely a school of thought that contended with others. This reduction was not due to Harrington alone, nor does Harrington represent or reflect any class or category of thinkers. His deviation from Aristotle is his own, like, and unlike, others.

The *Oceana*, in connection with the balance as an empirical criterion, contains normative elements for classification that bear a great similarity to those of Aristotle. Harrington also linked concepts to achieve his purpose but he did so differently. Aristotle's *Politics* is, despite the recognition of the importance of property in connection with citizenship, government, and law, a hymn in praise of love and friendship. After Aristotle describes a state based upon the ownership of property, a state in which shares of power and the right to participate in politics are allocated in proportion to ownership, he asserts that "a state is something more than an investment; its purpose is not merely to provide a living but to make a life that is worthwhile." This worthwhile life can only be found in associations that are characterized by love, "for it is our love of others that causes us to prefer life in a society . . ."[14]

Harrington began, not with an inquiry into the nature of the good life, but with stability—its benefits, its conditions, and its natural enemies. "We must ask," he seems to say, "to what degree a government must rely on force in order to rule?" The presupposition is that force is an unstable base upon which to build an orderly political system, and that, to the degree that force ceases to be a last resort for those in power and becomes the *only* recourse they have, the political system will become more unstable. Force was the most necessary and the most proximate means for maintaining order when the foundation of government, the distribution of property or the balance, did not match the allocation of power. For instance, if the people held the preponderance, an "overbalance" Harrington sometimes calls it, while the government remains in the hands of a king, the situation would be unstable. This monarch, because the people would not be dependent on him for food, would employ his army and coercive force in order to keep what was his. This army, because it was a great beast that had to be fed, would require great revenues and a source of supply. Without sufficient property, the health and efficiency of this great beast would decline; the king would be left without support. The people, no longer subject to a necessity that compelled obedience, would for a while suffer the coercion of the army. The gentler necessity would be replaced by force, a much harsher necessity; and, when visited upon a people with property in their hands, the means for throwing off this yoke would soon be employed. This method of governing is a perversion of the form of monarchy; it is a tyranny because of its dependence on force and its resulting instability. The same incongruity of balance to the form of government would make an aristocracy into an oligarchy and a commonwealth into anarchy. Any of these corrupt forms would be of short duration: "Each of which confusions, the balance standing otherwise, is but of short continuance, because against the nature of the balance, which, not destroyed, destroys that which opposes it."[15]

Two possibilities for change exist in the case described above. The people with the power that comes from having a preponderance of the property might replace their king-tyrant with the necessary commonwealth and thereby bring the form back into congruity with the balance. Or, if the king-tyrant moved first, he might use his army to seize three-fourths of the property from its present owners and thus succeed in adapting the balance to the monarchical form. The initial impression that Harrington is an early economic determinist may be discouraged by the theoretical existence of two possibilities instead of one. The inevitability of a change that produces a unity of balance and form remains a basic part of the theory, and change is certainly an inevitability that is determined by the ownership of property.

It cannot be denied that there is a soupçon of voluntarism within this determinism; however, Harrington definitely believed the first alternative—the people's adjusting the form to match the balance—to be more likely than, and morally superior to, the second—seizure by the king-tyrant. The art of lawgiving, he writes in another place, can be either true or false. True lawgiving consists in erecting political superstructures in conformity with the balance, and such law is true or good because it requires no force or violence. Because it requires the use of force and violence, the reduction of the balance to arbitrary superstructures is false lawgiving.[16] Clearly, when the balance and the form are not in harmony, the situation is fraught with ugly possibilities. Even promises made under other circumstances are no longer valid; for Harrington argues in the *Oceana* that the citizen is under no obligation to obey when the government does not correspond to the balance.[17] Neither is the king, or other rulers, bound under old laws any longer. Every person in the state, and nature itself, moves to a resolution of the problem. The balance and the superstructure must come together.

Harrington's typology includes six forms of government thus far: monarchy, mixed monarchy, and commonwealth are the good forms; tyranny, oligarchy, and anarchy, the bad forms. "But there be certain other confusions which being rooted in the balance are of longer continuance, and of worse consequence. . . ."[18] Two additional corrupt forms fall into this category, and the problem with respect to both of these is the absence of any individual or group capable of holding the preponderance of property. In other words, the power to settle the matter of what the form should be simply does not exist. The plight of a nation under these conditions is doubly unfortunate. Not only is the form out of touch with the balance, but the balance doesn't exist. When the nobility or aristocracy—a few, let us say—own half the property, and when the people own the other half, the only cure for the illness is the slow and often painful process by which one side "eats out" the other and gathers the preponderance to itself. In other instances in which the king has held half of the property and the people the other half, the government becomes a "shambles" and exists in confusion. In either instance, the horror of the form will continue until a balance can be created and until the king, the nobility, or the people emerge as the chief propertyowners. This process will always create misery, but to turn away from it is impossible. If a nation could avoid the task, the avoidance itself would cause greater problems since no government worth the name is possible until the want of a balance is satisfied.

When Harrington's desire for stability led him to consider the kinds of property, land, money, or goods in reference to their inherent ability to contribute order and predictability to the balance, money and goods were considered to be inferior to land. Because of the ease with which these could be exchanged and the rapidity with which they could be accumulated, they are dangerous as the basis for the balance in a commonwealth, though not so much so in a monarchy or mixed monarchy. In a commonwealth, the number of people involved in government and participating in the economic life of the state creates conditions where the volatile nature of money and goods can menace stability if they are unregulated by a dictatorial power. Since land changes hands more slowly and since its expense usually makes amassing it difficult, it possesses, in Harrington's opinion, built-in limitations that make it less dangerous than money or goods in any good form of government.

Nevertheless, in a commonwealth, the form of government in which land is most widely distributed, exchange and ownership of land must be limited and regulated if the balance is to remain appropriate to the form of the commonwealth.

The devices that Harrington proposes to counter the proximate danger of great fortunes in money and goods, as well as the more remote danger of great fortunes in land, are justified by the principle of the balance and by the value, in an orderly state, of stability. This desire for order explains why Harrington always seems more comfortable when he considers property in land: it is, for him, the chief and most valuable constituent in the balance. In "Preliminaries I," we read, ". . . because to property producing an empire, it is requir'd that it should have some root or foothold, which, except in land, it cannot have, being otherwise as it were upon the wing."[19] Harrington was aware that there were commonwealths in Holland and Italy that depended upon money and goods, and he had praise for them; but he also recognized that they had no choice as to what they would use as a foundation: they were small places possessing only a little territory, and they were forced to depend upon trade and commerce to build up the wealth needed for power.

The second variety of empire or dominion is that which Harrington called "foreign." He was alive, as others before him were, to the possibility that the establishment of colonies in conquered territories might not be the best way of maintaining the conquest. The chief danger in this policy was the tendency of the best people and natural leaders who were settlers to succumb to ambition and to mount independence movements. Harrington first established the difference between the balance at home and the balance abroad. "It has bin said, that national or independent empire, of what kind soever, is to be exercis'd by them that have the proper balance of dominion in the nation; wherfore provincial or dependent empire is not to be exercis'd by them that have the balance of dominion in the province, because that would bring the government from provincial and dependent, to national and independent."[20] The possibility that the balance might work to the disadvantage of the mother country is clear, ". . . wheras the richest among the provincials, tho native subjects, or citizens that have bin transplanted, are least admitted to the government abroad; for men, like flowers or roots being transplanted, take after the soil wherin they grow." Basing his advice on the experience of

Turkey in Egypt and of Venice and Spain in the Indies, Harrington thought it was not wise to allow colonists to participate in the governing of the area.

If it is not wise to allow either the native or the transplanted propertyowners to govern, upon what power should the ruling of the province be based? Perhaps it would be advisable for the entire property of the province to be taken away from its owners and for its possession and its use to be placed in the hands of governors sent from the mother country. Harrington considered this possibility with little enthusiasm. Such expropriations would be easy only if the province was held by a few propertyowners. Then this action would yield great advantage. In places where the people have equal shares, "the confiscation of many coms to little, and is not only dangerous but fruitless."[21] Neither action will make it possible to rely upon the balance in governing. Governing a foreign province will always be a matter of the ability of the occupying army, the governors, the superiority of the conquering race, or of the lack of experience of the native people in governing themselves or fighting.

This reliance on power raises another question: in view of the normative criteria used in dividing regimes into good and bad at home, does Harrington apply the same criteria in regard to provincial regimes that rest, not upon the balance, but upon force and coercion instead? In a slightly different context, Harrington responded candidly to this question in *The Art of Lawgiving:* "However, the possibility in a commonwealth of tyrannizing over provinces, is not to be cur'd; for be the commonwealth or the prince a state or a man after God's own heart, there is no way of holding a province but by arms."[22] Even the best of the good regimes will be forced by circumstances to be a bad government in any province that it holds. Coercion and its attendant instability will always be characteristic of foreign empire.

III   *Intellectual Origins of the Balance*

The principles of the balance, explained by Harrington in reference to both foreign and domestic politics, did not come to him unsuggested by other political thinkers. In "Preliminaries I," Harrington specifically mentions three of his predecessors who anticipated him without coming close enough to the basic idea to deny him the credit of his discovery. The three, Bacon, Machiavelli, and Aristotle, all wrote about the relationship of property and power without ever making the simple identification of the two that we find in Harrington and in many later writers and thinkers. Their failure in this respect, whether it originates in a conscious refusal or in some lack of mental penetration, is the difference between them and Harrington and the ground upon which he criticizes them.

There is also, in the same section of the *Oceana*, a rather thorough critique, given its brevity, of the definition and treatment of power found in Thomas Hobbes' *Leviathan*. This section of the "Preliminaries" is an assertion of basic principles of government; it contains homage to those thinkers who had a proper understanding of politics, and it views the formulation of the balance as an improvement, or a finishing touch, to a theory that, in an imperfect form could be traced back to the Greeks. The balance was also a rejection of, and a correction to, Hobbes and his theories.

Harrington found Hobbes, whom he styled "Leviathan" in the *Oceana*, hopelessly unrealistic when dealing with power: "Wherfore Leviathan, tho he be right where he says that riches are power, is mistaken where he says that prudence, or the reputation of prudence, is power: for the learning or prudence of a man is no more power than the learning or prudence of a book or author, which is properly authority."[23] The distinction that Harrington makes between the two is that in the case of those that have riches, as mentioned above, people have no choice but are subject to them out of necessity; with regard to those that have prudence, or its appearance, people are not compelled to submit to them but can freely choose to ignore or reject them. A foolish man may have power but no authority or prudence; yet he will still govern.

On another level, Harrington accused Hobbes of additional confusion. After quoting a particularly famous section of *Leviathan*—"The opinion that any monarch receiveth his Power by Covenant, that is to say on Condition, proceedeth from want of understanding this easie truth, that Covenants being but words, and breath, have no force to oblige, contain, constrain or protect any man, but what it has from the publique sword"[24]—Harrington observed that this "publique sword" must be held by a hand; it is not some power apart from the context in which it will be wielded. "The hand which holds this sword is the militia of a nation; and the militia is either an army in the field, or ready for the field upon occasion." Harrington took the abstract concept of power and united it with what he believed to be its material foundation. It is the army, and it is the same army that depends upon the land for food and other supplies. To the extent that Hobbes could not see this connection, his theory was empirically inadequate. On two counts Hobbes is found wanting; and in both instances his inability to move beyond the mere idea of power and to examine its true nature excites Harrington's criticism. Later, in regard to commonwealths, we will find Harrington replying to Hobbes on other points at odds between them.

Harrington professed to find the first traces of the balance in the writings of Sir Francis Bacon, especially in the Twenty-Ninth Essay, where Bacon advised all states that had ambitions for glory to be careful about encouraging the rapid and unhealthy growth of the nobility and gentry. Bacon believed that too many lords and gentlemen caused the common subjects to become no more than base servants who were unfit to bear arms and that this decline would most adversely affect the infantry "which is the nerve of an army." This harping, as Harrington put it, of Bacon upon an un-tuned string is really the balance of dominion or property. In the text cited above, Bacon has made a mistake; for Harrington be-lieved that it does not necessarily follow, as Bacon has made it, that an increase in the number of landowners, if this includes both noblemen and gentlemen, will inevitably cause a decline in the quality of the nation's commons and, because of this, in its arms too.

To Harrington, Bacon came closer to the truth of the balance when he praised Henry VII for developing a class of husbandmen on the land with holdings sufficient to keep them in plenty and to remove the necessity that had made them the servants of others. This class of men, both Bacon and Harrington agreed, forms the backbone of an army and a nation. Harrington, without relating the fact of ownership to any group, made the point that increasing the number of owners will inevitably increase the number of good soldiers, gentlemen, commoners, or whatever. This factor was probably something that neither Bacon nor the king anticipated: "for where the owner of the plow coms to have the sword too, he will use it in defence of his own. . . ."[25] In this statement Harrington means that increasing the number of good soldiers will have the effect of changing the balance, of changing whatever ex-isted before into a commonwealth; and this change, of course, would not ordinarily be in the interest of a monarch.

Even before Bacon wrote, Machiavelli had noted much the same relationship between property and power. But, "Machiavel has miss'd it very narrowly and more dangerously; for not fully perceiving that if a commonwealth be gall'd by the gentry, it is by their over balance. . . ."[26] Harrington's specific reference here is to Book I, Chapter 55 of Machiavelli's *The Discourses*, in which the problem of "corruption" in commonwealths is described. The interdependence of civic virtue, equality, and the republican, or commonwealth, form of government is clearly stated. Where civic virtue, by which Machiavelli means the ability to see one's own interest and the interest of the state as one and the same, is widespread among the citizenry and where considerable equality exists, it is possible to establish a republic. In the same community, it would be impossible to set up a principality. Where the citizenry has become corrupt—where they do not make an identification between their own and the state's interests, where they have lost their respect for religion, where they refuse to pay their taxes and do not observe the laws—the establishment and maintenance of a republic becomes an impossibility.

Machiavelli believed that an important first step in the downward movement toward corruption is an increasing reliance on foreign trade. An influx of foreign goods cause dissatisfaction, weakens self-sufficiency, and promotes the popularity of foreign customs. A second great cause of corruption is a class of lords or gentry, for they "live in idleness on the abundant revenue derived from their estates, without having anything to do either with their cultivation or with other forms of labour essential to life."[27] Men of this rank who have subjects of their own as well as castles to command are an even more pernicious threat to civic virtue and the commonwealth, ". . . for men born in such conditions are inimical to any form of civic government." All that can be done in a state with such a class of men, since laws are not sufficient to maintain order among them, is to establish a much superior force, such as might be associated with a king, to restrain their ambitions.

Corruption is a condition with specific causes; of these causes, the inequality constituted by the existence of what may be considered a leisure class is most serious. Machiavelli recognized the importance of land in this problem. It was land ownership that made this leisure class possible and maintained it. And Machiavelli recognized the relationship between the form of government and its foundation in property when he advised princes interested in establishing monarchies where a condition of equality exists to select ambitious and restless men and to convert them into gentry or nobility by giving them castles and land. For Machiavelli, kings and gentry go hand in hand. For Harrington, they do not.

On the other side of this coin, the relationship between the gentry and the commons, or the people, in Harrington's terms, is the point at issue between Harrington and Machiavelli. Machiavelli believed that gentry and people were natural enemies. To him, every society was divided between those few who were ambitious and sought, first of all, to gain positions of dominance, and the many who wished only to pursue their own livelihood in an atmosphere of safety and security unhindered by the few. As a result of this division, the few, or gentry, and the many, the people, could never be at peace with one another. Harrington disagreed: in Switzerland, the gentry were admired by the people, and both classes cooperated in maintaining a healthy commonwealth. Harrington granted the gentry some variety in their relationship with the people. These could be either friendly or unfriendly. An unfriendly gentry was a great danger to a popular government, but a friendly gentry was the heart and soul of a popular government. The attitude of gentry and people in regard to one another was determined, not by deeply seated unchanging and incompatible ambitions, but by the distribution of property. A gentry possessing the preponderance of property would be hostile; but, in a state in which the people held the preponderance and the gentry were an elite of talented men instead of powerful men, the gentry would be friendly. In like manner the relationship between a king and the nobility or gentry would be determined by the balance.[28]

The question of where such attitudes originated led to the heart of the disagreement between Machiavelli and Harrington about the corruption of the people. Machiavelli was quite forceful when he said that a corrupt people are unequal to the task of supporting a commonwealth. He provided a convincing description of such a people: they are irreligious, tax-dodging, luxury-loving, cowardly, selfish, and mean-spirited. He was equally forceful when he described the evils that naturally flow from this corruption: conspiracy, disorder, treason, and rebellion. Harrington does not disagree with any of these views; but, when Machiavelli offered reasons, in various and diverse places in *The Discourses*, for such corruption, Harrington was moved to his sharpest criticism. Inequality of wealth, noted above as a cause of corruption in the people, was not the only cause that Machiavelli cited. So far as corruption in many of the Italian city states was concerned, Machiavelli blamed the Roman Catholic church, and the example set by its court, for the decline of public-spiritedness. In other places, bad customs developed during many generations were the cause of corruption; but in any state, the forced or voluntary reliance upon auxiliaries or mercenaries for military was not only a sign but a cause of corruption.

To Harrington, Machiavelli appeared in these explanations to be very close to the theoretical breakthrough that would explain and unify thought about healthy and unhealthy commonwealths and the nature of the foundation of such governments. Instead of pushing forward to the final reduction, Machiavelli had created a maze of causes that left the origin, or chief source, of such corruption shrouded in doubt. Harrington simplified the problem and the answer by reducing all of these causes to an analysis of the balance:

> A People [says Machiavel] that is corrupt, is not capable of a commonwealth. But in shewing what a corrupt people is, he has either involved himself, or me; nor can I otherwise com out of the labyrinth, than by saying, the balance altering a people, as to the foregoing government, must of necessity be corrupt: but corruption in this sense signifys no more than that the corruption of one government [as in natural bodys] is the generation of another. Wherfore if the balance alters from monarchy, the corruption of the people in this case is that which makes them capable of a commonwealth. But wheras I am not ignorant, that the corruption which he means is in manners, this also is from the balance. For the balance leading from monarchical into popular, abates the luxury of the nobility, and, inriching the people, brings the government from a more privat to a more public interest; which coming nearer, as has bin shewn, to justice and right reason, the people upon a like alteration is so far from such corruption of manners, as should render them incapable of a commonwealth, that of necessity they must thereby contract such a reformation of manners as will bear no other kind of government.[29]

Harrington's reduction of public morality or civic virtue and its opposing vices to the place where they are simply a function of the balance is a type of determinism that is foreign to the theory of Machiavelli. In this failure to recognize the relationship between property and power, Harrington believed that Machiavelli had failed as an observer and theorist. What had, for Machiavelli, seemed to be a failure in character was, for Harrington, a flaw in the economic and political structure of society that, of necessity, corrupted and made the people miserable.

This basic misconception on Machiavelli's part was cited by Harrington as the reason for the faulty analysis of the decline of Rome found in *The Discourses* and for Machiavelli's inability to see the possibility of an immortal and perfect commonwealth and the promise, implicitly stated in the more confident sections of Harrington's writings, that mankind can control the course of history.

Aristotle is the third thinker to which Harrington refers in his initial elaboration of the balance. As Harrington indelicately puts it, "You have Aristotle full of it in divers places, especially where he says, that immoderate wealth, as where one man or a few have greater possessions than the equality or the frame of the commonwealth will bear. . . ."[30] This reference to Aristotle concerns the part of *The Politics* that refers to the causes of revolution and sedition in a commonwealth. Immoderate wealth is one cause of these misfortunes in a list of seven that includes profit, dignity, cruelty, fear, contemptuous attitudes, and disproportionate aggrandizement; but other minor causes are also mentioned. All of these are considered, not only in terms of their effect on the stability of the state, but also in regard to the character of the men who are susceptible to such temptations. The fault lies not only in the conditions but also in the soul of the individual.[31] And for Aristotle a description of the conditions that are likely to produce revolution is never limited to the balance.

Aristotle, to Harrington, suffered therefore from the same lack of penetration that was the lot of Bacon and Machiavelli. Indeed, in each case, the earlier theorists that speculated about the degree to which power depended on property were unwilling to claim what Harrington claimed, and their speculation about this matter remained only a part of their general theories. The prominence that Harrington gives them in the "Preliminaries" may indicate that each theorist provided him with insights that formed the basis for his own theory of the balance or that he wished to use one or more of these predecessors to lend support to his own theory. If any of the three is to be selected as exercising the predominate influence, the choice must be Machiavelli. For the reference by Harrington to his works was more thorough and systematic; his praise of him was more fulsome; and his references to Aristotle and Bacon were briefer and much less conclusive, and were used to corroborate the main point that Harrington wishes to make about property and power, the foundation and superstructure. Of more importance is

Harrington's attack on, and criticism of, Thomas Hobbes. Two most obvious influences in this early statement of the balance, one negative, the other generally positive, were Thomas Hobbes and Niccolo Machiavelli. The balance was developed as a refutation of Hobbes and as the perfecting of Machiavelli.

IV *Weighing the Balance*

Once stated in the opening pages of the *Oceana*, the theory of the balance underwent no real changes in Harrington's later works. Though Harrington was forced to defend his theory and to elaborate it again and again, and though he used it on many occasions as a tool for social and political analysis, he never weakened it by depriving it of the force it had gained from its rigorous reduction of the source of all power to the ownership of property. The initial response, critical but not hostile, to the *Oceana* came from Dr. H. Ferne, a clergyman who took exception to some of the things Harrington wrote about religion and the church. There were other matters upon which Harrington and this critic disagreed, and they entered into a correspondence. After several exchanges, consisting of questions asked of Dr. Ferne by Harrington, Ferne's answers, and Harrington's responses, the correspondence was published in January 1657. This Harrington pamphlet, entitled *Pian Piano*, included a question concerning the balance posed by Harrington, "Whether Men, as they become richer or poorer, free or servile, be not of a different Genius, or become new model'd; and whether these things happen not as the Balance changes?"[32] When Dr. Ferne replied that he would leave sudden changes in the genius and nature of man to the "pipe of Orpheus," this comment provoked Harrington to term the doctor's reply, "A pretty jeer" and to assert that such a change would not be, or had not been, sudden; it could easily take a hundred and forty years in its accomplishment.

In this exchange, the balance, in particular its profound effect on the genius or even on the nature of man, is asserted with some clarity by Harrington; and he indicated that the inevitability of adjusting the superstructure to the foundation need not be revolutionary but, on the basis of available experience, may be evolutionary. Harrington, as was often the case in the controversies that he excited and which excited him, could not resist, in connection with Ferne's answer, drawing a little additional blood. When he remarked that, with the alteration of the balance in England, the

clergy were losing both land and power, Harrington reminded
Ferne that, "The butcher sought his knife, and had it in his
mouth."

When Harrington considered another aspect of the balance in
The Prerogative of Popular Government (1658), he posed in the
third chapter of this work the question of whether the balance of
dominion in land was the natural cause of empire. His answer
asserted that the principle was particularly easy to demonstrate:
people with money could hire other people to do their bidding. In a
reference that any statesman in sixteenth century Europe would understand, Harrington said, "but no mony, no Switzers, as the
French speak: if the mony be flown, so are the men also."[33] What is
needed, beyond the ability to exploit a necessary dependence of the
poor upon the rich, is a continually productive source of wealth:
"Whence a bank never paid an army; paying an army, soon became
no bank. But where a prince or a nobility has an estate in land, the
revenue whereof will defray this charge, there their men are
planted, have toes that have roots, and arms that bring forth what
fruit you please." Harrington has, in answer to additional criticism,
not only restated the importance of dependency and necessity in
politics but also strengthened the bias inherent in the balance in
favor of landed property over property in money and goods.

Money does, however, serve the purpose as well or better in certain specific situations. As noted earlier, money and goods are more
than an adequate foundation for power in those places where
property in land is not sufficient or has not yet been introduced.
Since other states that are really no more than cities that exist by
trade have insufficient territory for the feeding of the people or an
army, the maintenance of the people cannot then rest upon land
and its produce but upon the revenue that comes from trade. In
other words, these states will be dominated by money rather than
by land no matter how the land is divided; and, where only one
arrangement is possible, that one arrangement is best.

In the situation in which money is at least as good as land as a
basis for power (in what Harrington calls "narrow countries" where
the land is scant and not very productive), a potentially dangerous
situation exists, since neither money nor land can gain a legitimate
superiority but only contend with each other. Since not much can
be done to strengthen the position of the landed propertyowner in
such a situation, those with money will be tempted to use various
means to destroy the position of landed property in the balance. For

this reason, "narrow countries" must exercise greater care than others in controlling the methods of moneylenders. This control did not extend to the forbidding of lending and usury but only to the use of these techniques in ways that would undermine the holding of small plots. These allowances, which acknowledge the adaptation of the balance to differing conditions, constitute an important refinement of the theory. Land remains the firmest basis upon which to build an army and a state, but recognition is given the positive role in politics of money and goods.[34]

The Prerogative of Popular Government contains another rebuttal that Harrington made to his critics. He had been brought to task for making the dependence of one person upon another too much a matter of riches, for his critics thought that obedience might actually come from any number of other motivations and that one who relied upon wealth alone to gain the allegiance and support others would be disappointed. This view is true, Harrington agreed, if the person who is asked to obey has money of his own. Whatever is owned dependently, however, is owed to the landlord and is his to command. Not having things makes men obedient; having things makes them independent. Harrington says that under conditions of poverty and want even the wise serve the unwise in order to survive.[35]

During the year following the publication of *The Prerogative*, Harrington wrote and published another exposition of his ideas, *The Art of Lawgiving*, which begins with another forthright statement of the balance in its first chapter: "The distribution of property, so far as it regards the nature or procreation of government, lys in the over balance of the same. . . ." Harrington also noted that "Imperfections of the balance, that is, where it is not good or down weight, cause imperfect governments; as those of the Roman and of the Florentin people, and those of the Hebrew kings and Roman emperors, being each exceedingly bloody, or at least turbulent."[36] Although nothing has yet been said by Harrington that is new, he then proceeds to unite the guiding principle of the Stuart kings—divine right—with his own theory of the balance: "Wherever, thro causes unforeseen by human providence, the balance comes to be intirely chang'd, it is the more immediately to be attributed to Divine Providence: and since God cannot will the necessary cause, but he must also will the necessary effect or consequence, what government soever is in the necessary direction of the balance, the same is of Divine right."

This statement is an important inflation of Harrington's claims; and, though it was probably not universally persuasive, it may have denied the more extreme Monarchists of one of their main arguments, or at least, perhaps, blunted its effectiveness. It is, of course, common enough to see whatever presently exists as the conscious and positive product of divine will and to use this identification to buttress the status quo and to create counterpressure to any change. Harrington came to see the balance as an inevitable congruity of foundation and superstructure, a law of nature, a necessity; and he believed that the hand of God might be seen in this congruity, at least by those who needed to see it in order to believe in the existence or truth of the balance.

We may note that these references in later works by Harrington to the balance are still statements of a general principle couched in different terms that are adjusted only slightly in order to clarify the theory or, on other occasions, to deflect or answer criticism. When Harrington first wrote, he had already considered his theory fully and it needed no real additional development. To the end of his career as a pamphleteer and thinker, he continued to say of the balance what he had said in *Oceana*. He argued, sometimes very effectively, that it was a law that could not be safely ignored, that it was a law that had always applied in politics and would always apply, that it was a law of nature that could be scientifically demonstrated and a law that emanated from God Himself.

Harrington's life and reputation were complicated by men who could not or did not see the theory of the balance in the same way. Not only was the theory attacked as an oversimplification, but Harrington's use of it to analyze the contemporary situation in England was not accepted by many as accurate. These reactions and the criticisms they spawned are still with us. Trying to discover the origin of the balance has led scholars in our own time to look beyond Harrington's statement of the theory and his attempt to place the theory in the tradition of Aristotle and Machiavelli, in order to find some other source of the idea. A survey of the various sources proposed by these scholars indicates that there is no end here to the variety encountered already in regard to Harrington. The search for this source, like the search for the source of the Nile, takes us over interesting and exotic terrain, intellectual or literary in this case; and it also arouses occasionally intense disputes that involve not only the explorers themselves but even those who are only interested in exploration and explorers.

Richard Henry Tawney, a comparatively early entrant in these lists, thought that Harrington's theory of the balance was based on a careful observation of social and economic change in England during the two centuries preceding the civil war. According to Tawney, Harrington chose to communicate his theory in metaphors that he borrowed from business accountancy. Words such as "balance," "overbalance," "equipoise," and "counterpoise" are cited as evidence that Harrington stood in the middle of an intellectual movement that dates back to the sixteenth century when G. de Malynes first applied such terms to trade. Later, Sir Thomas Overbury, in the early years of the reign of James I, used this particular vocabulary when he discussed power relationships among states; and, at approximately the same time, Bacon expanded the application of these metaphors to include an analysis of society in general. Cromwell himself spoke in terms of a "balance" and again made reference to the need in England for a system of "balancing power." Harrington used words, then, that were not new but that were, in Tawney's opinion, "firmly fixed in current usage." In addition to Harrington's own acknowledged debt to Aristotle, Machiavelli, and Bacon, there is this—a vocabulary derived from the world of business, generalized to the point where it became the mode in which people communicated their ideas about politics, a necessary accessory to the climate of opinion in Harrington's England.[37]

To Charles Blitzer, "The notion of equilibrium, of balance, was taken directly from physics; in order to demonstrate the relevance to politics of this notion it was necessary, somehow, to reduce the elements of political life to a form that would admit of quantitative expression and of measurement on a common scale."[38] The close affinity of concepts of equilibrium, balance, stability is undeniable and so, too, is the degree of success experienced by accountants, economists, and physicists in establishing these terms as descriptions of the natural, normal, and even optimal conditions of that part of reality that attracts their attention. The temptation to gain for politics the "quantitative expression" and the "measurement on a common scale" that had already apparently been gained in accountancy, economics, and physics was probably too great to be withstood. The confident belief in the existence of a "common scale" developed before Albert Einstein destroyed the absolute authority of Newtonian physics and before the various economic and social upheavals called into question the theories of so many scholars about the naturalness of stability and balance.

Harrington had, in passing, paid his respects to William Harvey in his first description of the balance. This and other statements in which Harrington linked his discovery with those of Harvey prompted Blitzer to observe that anatomy served Harrington as "the proper model for the new science of politics." Not only was the method of Harvey, observation and induction, most acceptable to Harrington, but in medicine the concept of "balance" was thought to be at the root of all illness and all cures.

J. G. A. Pocock attributed the balance to Harrington's knowledge of the feudal system. It was not so much the changes‚ in land ownership that moved Harrington to reflection but the Medieval network of obligations owed by vassals to their lords. He dealt with economics only to the extent that it was concerned with land ownership, and he dealt with land ownership to the degree that it determined the obligations of one person to another. These obligations interested him because they would, again in keeping with the medieval system, have a great deal to do with the owning, maintaining, and bearing of arms. Arms would always be the final arbiter in politics for Harrington. And Harrington was sustained in these conclusions when he studied the institutions of Greece and Rome.[39]

H. R. Trevor-Roper argued that the balance is perhaps a metaphysical concept "like the signature of the Social Contract" and that it could not possibly be developed out of any accurate observation of events or movements afoot in England from the fifteenth century on. To Trevor-Roper, the concept was essentially ideological, but it was the product of a mind perfectly in tune with the interests and thinking of a particular class, the gentry. The balance, in this interpretation, serves a specific purpose—it justifies the gaining and holding of political power by the lesser gentry, Republican to a man, and long fenced off from the mainstream of English power by its geographic isolation from the court and by the monopoly in offices held by the nobility and greater gentry. Trevor-Roper is persuasive when he says that the real distribution of land, money, and goods in England when Harrington wrote did not favor the gentry or the people. Because of this situation, Trevor-Roper contends that most contemporary supporters of Harrington's doctrine were not so much confirming his observations as supporting his dogma.[40]

Felix Raab wondered how Harrington had discovered the balance. "What was there," he asked, "in Harrington's experience of the world (both at first and at second hand) which might have led him to the formulation of such an idea."[41] He decided that Harrington's life was rich and varied enough to provide him with all that was needed to produce the principle of the balance. Personal experience was not, perhaps, what was most important. Raab was convinced that Harrington needed a principle like the balance in order "to derive from English history the republican certainty and necessity which his political alignment demanded." In this version of how the theory developed, Harrington set a goal and then ransacked his own first and secondhand experiences for the analytical tool that will serve his purpose best. In short, the balance was an ex post facto development, a practical discovery by a practical man.

Harrington, himself, in the "Preliminaries" has already given us a survey of his secondhand experience. He was quite willing to cite authorities in partial or indirect support of his ideas. What we are left in doubt about is whether they were read or "experienced" before, during, or after Harrington had made his discovery. Students find, in their studies, confirmation for, or a challenge to, what they have already experienced and determined as valid. They may also, of course, find both confirmation and challenge in their studies. We have, however, the expectation that, whatever the sequence, the student will not be the same person at the end of this experience as at the beginning. Either convictions will be held more strongly or a new search will begin.

Some resolution, inadequate probably, to the questions raised about Harrington's response to what he read in the books of other thinkers can be found in a careful account of what we know of Harrington's life, the primary context of his work.

CHAPTER 2

Harrington in His Own Time

I *The Problem of Context*

TO many scholars who have studied Harrington, the relationship between his life and his theories seems direct and uncomplicated. William T. Bluhm has written that, "We have seen . . . that the everyday nonscientific experience of a writer is frequently an important source of his political theories. This is certainly true in Harrington's case. His boyhood observations of life in Lincolnshire may well have suggested to him the importance of economics for political power, and his concept of the balance of property."[1] Charles Blitzer is even more certain: "James Harrington clearly belongs in the class of political theorists whose ideas were shaped by the pressure of personal and historical circumstances."[2] While Bluhm and Blitzer agree that Harrington's formative years in the English countryside shaped his perception of essential human relationships, Blitzer places more emphasis on Harrington's family background and on the development of its position in society, as well as on the apparent rise to eminence in England of many others in the same social and economic circumstances.

We have already recognized that the balance was presented in the *Oceana* in its final form. The intellectual process that produced this idea cannot be traced in any of Harrington's earlier works; it was finished before 1656, the year *Oceana* was published. If we look for the origin of the balance in the life and times of Harrington, we must restrict ourselves to the period prior to 1656 and begin with the question, "What experiences can we reasonably expect Harrington to have had?" We may then be moved to ask, "Which of these experiences would Harrington have retained and allowed to affect the way he viewed and reflected upon political reality?" These are particularly difficult questions since Harrington has not left us an autobiography, letters, or a diary. This lack of material is a

38

serious handicap; for, without such revealing sources, we must depend upon a variety of interesting fragments to reconstruct Harrington's early years.

There are perils in such a venture for the scholar. Because much that has all the tinkling but none of the timbre of scholarship has been done on such projects, two commentators on Harrington have advised against excess. To J. G. A. Pocock, the greatest danger is the tendency to argue in a circle—to assume that we know with certainty the social position or class membership of a theorist; to relate the theorist's ideas to the interests, aims, and experiences of that social class; and to establish a claim to social significance for the theorist. It is then possible to repeat this process in reverse to determine beyond all questions the real purpose, loyalty, and class membership of the theorist. Pocock, who has seen this process used, calls it " . . . a thoroughly deplorable perversion of critical method," for he thinks that this exercise comes from assuming that the relationship of ideas to social reality is direct and obvious.[3] This relationship is not direct and obvious, though perhaps the apparent congruity of these in Harrington's case constitutes an exception to the usual.

Judith Shklar introduces, in connection with Harrington, another doubt in the face of scholarly claims to certainty. After comparing the interpretations of Trevor-Roper and Tawney, which are at odds and at the center of the modern controversy over Harrington and the Balance, she indicated that individuals must be regarded as more than "social types" and that there was a great deal more to the study of ideas than the identification of ideological processes. The conflict over Harrington and the origin and purpose of his ideas had originated in the larger dispute between those who study social history and those who study the history of ideas. Ideas are part of group life and are impersonal to the social historians. Ideas are "the expressions of individual thinkers who communicate directly and personally with their predecessors, contemporaries and us," assert those who study the history of ideas.[4] Professor Shklar thinks there need be no quarrel between these two ways of looking at the past, but we need to bear in mind that each asks different questions and gets different answers—and they often do so about the same thinker. If contemporary scholarship has erred, however, it has seemed to err, in Professor Shklar's opinion, in favor of social history: "It is the habit of personifying events, ages, nations, classes

and other groups, indeed history itself, that has led to the deper-
sonalizing of individuals."

There is little doubt that we are led to expect that the ideas held
by people are produced by a rather predictable and even con-
trollable process—by socialization, to put a modern name on it.
When we encounter, in person or in writing, someone who does not
satisfy this expectation we are surprised and then, perhaps, angry or
frightened. The modern discipline of social history was not needed
to produce this conditioning; it has been a mainstay of societies for
centuries. In two important books that contain long sections on the
life of James Harrington, the same anecdote is used to make slightly
different points about the class and background of their subject.

"Good man! what moveth James Harrington to provoke the
wrath of kings? His own lineage is derived from the blood of the
Anointed."[5] This was the outraged question asked by an early critic
of *Oceana*. The rest of this letter, later published under the comment, "A slap on the snout of the republican swine," enumerates all
that the Harringtons had gained from their attachment to the same
monarchy that James Harrington wished to replace with a commonwealth. This list of advantages included a wedding gift, "The
great King Henry the Eighth matched his daughter to John
Harrington, and, though a bastard, dowered her with the rich lands
of Bath's priory"; important appointments, "Our blessed King
James did enoble your great uncle the Lord Harrington of Exton
and entrusted to his care and wisdom the renounced Princess
Elizabeth for tuition"; public displays of affection, "Yourself was
caressed by the blessed martyr Charles, and honored with his words,
and even his princely favors from his own hands on the scaffold,";
and gifts—a small golden toothpick case given to James Harrington,
again by the "blessed martyr Charles." The author of this appraisal,
J. Lesley, concluded his tirade: "If this be learning, give me to
know only righteousness, and seek the Lord by obeying those whom
he hath appointed."

When Charles Blitzer used this letter to introduce a survey of
Harrington's family and its history, his view was that James Harrington wrote against the principle of monarchy in general and, by
application, against England's royal house because he was formed
and shaped by, and even represented, a particular kind of people,
the gentry. Blitzer says, therefore, that we cannot understand
Harrington without understanding his family and what they
represented. For Blitzer and for Tawney, this class was steadily ris-

ing in power, wealth, and prestige through the fifteenth and sixteenth centuries.

Ian Grimble, who was mainly interested in the history of the
Harrington family and in James Harrington's political ideas as only
one member's accomplishments, views Lesley's letter slightly
differently. "It understood how a plain country gentleman of
modest means moved among kings from his youth up, without em-
barrassment or reverence. What its author failed to understand was
the traditional character of this irreverence. He had not considered
that a family closely related to kings for many centuries was more
likely to regard the sovereign as primus inter pares than the newly
enobled, and less likely to be impressed by a doctrine of divine
right."[6] Grimble's assorted Harringtons are not newly arrived and
anxious to be rid of a monarchy that thwarts their ambitions for
power and position. They've been close enough to the monarchy to
see behind the panoply and the public image. James Harrington,
the inheritor of this tradition of friendly irreverence, would be the
very one to recognize when the monarchy was no longer serving a
useful purpose and then to propose replacing it.

Despite the different uses to which Lesley's outburst has already
been put, there is one more point that we can use it to make. We
know for certain that Lesley was extremely angry at what
Harrington had written in favor of commonwealths and, by implica-
tion, against the house of Stuart. Lesley also evinces some surprise
in this anger, surprise that a member of such a well-placed family
could be so disloyal to the monarchy. There is no attempt to distinguish between rising and already risen gentry here. A man with
every advantage had attacked the very source of those advantages,
and he should be reminded that loyalty was the payment due.

Lesley's shocked anger is the result of expectations disappointed.
Lesley obviously knew not only the Harrington family but James
Harrington's place in it. On this knowledge he had based his idea of
what was proper in the way of political ideology and activity. James
Harrington had surprised him, and his reaction was sharp and
quick. In a sense, Harrington was a traitor to his king and his class
and, because England for men of Lesley's ilk was no more than king
and class, a traitor to his country, too. To translate Lesley's reaction
to our own time and vocabulary, we might say that he was struck by
the discrepancy between the context of Harrington's life and the
text of *Oceana*. When Lesley tries to find some cause for
Harrington's inexplicable behavior, he cannot find it in

Harrington's family background; he finds it, instead, in "learning"—the kind of learning that undermines and rejects the Bible, the church, and the other traditional verities of England. This is the "New Science" of Bacon and Galileo or, perhaps, it is the baleful influence of the Classics that Hobbes had thought to be the ruin of Harrington's generation. Our point is made: the anecdote may be used to prove that family and class had little to do with *Oceana*.

Without attempting to establish the validity of this early investigation of the source of Harrington's ideas, we may note that Lesley made an attempt to explain "What moveth James Harrington" and that his explanation implicitly rejected the contention that family background had any positive role in determining this. Lesley labored under two serious disadvantages as an analyst: he was a contemporary of Harrington's, and he could not avail himself of hindsight to the extent that modern scholars may; moreover, he was emotionally involved in the controversies, intellectual and political, that had torn England apart during the civil war. Without hindsight or dispassionate objectivity, an analysis has little to recommend it. It may still, against all odds, be correct. What remains, here, is that three writers, at the very least, start with Harrington's family when they try to locate the core of his thought. Though disagreement exists about how important a part of the context of the balance this influence is, we need to consider it.

II *Early Life and Career*

James Harrington was born at Upton, Northamptonshire, on the first Friday of January, 1611.[7] His father was Sir Sapcote Harrington, knight, of Rand, Lincolnshire, the nephew of Baron John Harrington; and his mother was Jane Samuell, daughter of Sir William Samuell of Upton. James Harrington was their first son and heir to a considerable fortune in land and income. By birth a member of a noble family of Rutlandshire, he was the great-grandson to Sir James Harrington, who was forebearer of eight dukes, three marquisses, seventy earls, twenty-seven viscounts, and thirty-six barons. This family "had helped to make and unmake kings, but never once had they held high office under the crown."[8]

The Harrington who grew up at the family seat in Rand is reported to have been an extremely intelligent child. To his parents, "he rather kept them in awe than needed their correction"; to Toland, he had a quick and ready wit and a facetious temper.[9]

Harrington apparently received his early education in his father's home, but he entered Trinity College, Oxford, as a gentleman commoner in 1629. When his father died during this first year at Oxford, James, the eldest son, inherited all of Sapcote Harrington's estates at age eighteen. Despite the continued existence of the court of wards, the institution that managed the estates of minors in the king's interest, James possessed a soccage tenure that enabled him to choose his guardian. He selected his maternal grandmother, the Lady Samuell, a particularly understanding and wise person, to perform this duty. It was she who granted him permission to withdraw from Oxford before he had earned a degree and allowed him to travel on the Continent in pursuit of a broader education.

When Harrington went first to Holland in 1632, he wanted to study military science, one of the occupations considered fit for a gentleman; for Holland had recently freed itself from Spanish control and had come to serve as a staging place for English efforts to intervene on the Protestant-French side in the Thirty Years War. He enlisted in the Earl of Craven's English Volunteer Regiment in hopes not only of learning the art of war but also of doing something useful in behalf of the Winter Queen of Bavaria, Elizabeth, the daughter of James I of England and the ward of Harrington's granduncle, Baron John Harrington. This unfortunate woman had married Frederick, the Elector Palatine, who had been deprived of the crown and of lands of the king of Bavaria, that were his by right, through action of the Holy Roman Emperor, the leader of the Catholic side in the Thirty Years War. It was the hope of regaining this inheritance that drew many English gentlemen to Holland and to the volunteer regiments. Harrington also had himself listed on the rolls of Sir Robert Stone's regiment, probably on the chance that, if one of the two regiments didn't make it into battle, the other would.

Because of the strong Harrington family connection with the Elector Palatine's family, James was welcome at their court. Although the English regiments did not see much action because the great military leader of the Protestant side, Gustavus Adolphus, rejected their offers of assistance, this inactivity meant that Harrington was free to make use of his welcome to learn the somewhat more peaceful art of politics. Harrington, described by all his contemporaries as a most amiable and amusing man, enlivened the court of the Elector Frederick and charmed and diverted the Winter Queen and her daughters. Frederick came to value his advice and companionship and took Harrington with him on an official visit to Denmark.

Following this interlude in his European travels, Harrington went to France, where the government impressed him with its efficiency. He disliked the political system, however, and the concentration of power it placed in the hands of one man. From France, Harrington journeyed to Rome; and, though he was essentially Protestant in religion, he was interested enough in the papacy to visit the Vatican. This interest did not mitigate the irreverence that Grimble believes was part of Harrington's inheritance; for, when Harrington was offered an opportunity to kiss the Pope's toe in exchange for a blessed candle, ordinarily a valued souvenir of such visits, he declined the privilege and missed the opportunity. Later, when he was serving as a member of the household of King Charles I, the king teased him about this refusal by saying that kissing the Pope's toe might be viewed as reasonable homage to a temporal prince, which in addition to his spiritual offices, was a position held by the pontiff. When Harrington replied that, having kissed the king's hand, he could not bring himself to kiss any other prince's toe, his answer pleased Charles very much.

From Rome, Harrington went to Venice where he spent a lengthy period of time; for this place impressed him the most. Venice was no longer at the peak of its power and prestige, nor was it any longer the republic that had been praised so fulsomely. Nevertheless, it was still a great city, the political hub of an empire of sorts, and a center of learning and culture. Harrington was a young man with a young man's penchant for enthusiasms, and Venice became one of these. He occupied his time in this "Serene Republic" reading and reflecting upon the histories of Machiavelli, Giannotti, and Contarini—all of which made much of Venice, its empire, its citizens and their republican virtue. That those who have read Harrington and the history of Venice have shown that his Venice no longer existed, that perhaps it had never existed, may be damaging to Harrington's reputation as an accurate observer of social and political reality, it is not a serious challenge to the contention that some imaginary Venice provided him with an inspiration and vision that remained with him throughout his life. When we examine Harrington's decided preference for commonwealths in more detail, the impact of the time spent there becomes obvious. Suffice it to say at this point that Harrington took the trouble to learn Italian and that he purchased numerous historical and political books in that language. He went from Venice to visit parts of Germany and returned home to England about 1637.

Because Harrington had attained his majority before his return, he was concerned at first with the management of his estates. He also assumed the responsibility of providing a living and education for his younger brother, three sisters, his stepmother, two stepbrothers, and two stepsisters, a duty he performed to the satisfaction of his biographers as well as his family. Harrington, comfortably well off, able because of this to live in London and at court, witty and well educated, widely traveled, made himself agreeable to King Charles and presently became a member of the privy chamber extraordinary. King Charles enjoyed his company, and Harrington went north with the royal forces when they went to reassert the king's control in Scotland during what is called the First Bishops' War.

By late summer 1641, with the tensions between Charles and Parliament growing, Harrington was back at Rand. On two occasions he loaned moderate sums of money to the government for the support of the campaigns that were then being conducted in Ireland against various rebels. It is reported, and accepted by some of his biographers, that Harrington stood unsuccessfully for Parliament in 1642. All that remains of the candidacy is a letter, written to the alderman of Stamford and his brethren by an untitled Harrington of approximately thirty years of age, that asks that the writer be considered for Parliament. The writer praises King Charles as a Solomon and calls England a republic. The signature is missing, but there is one revelatory sentence, "To you [the alderman] is commited both the sword, and the balance to divide and distinguish."[10] The concept and phrasing are Harringtonian, and the rest of the letter is written in the ornate and elaborate style that was characteristic of Harrington's later writing. In any event, it was shortly after this election that Harrington appeared before Parliament as the English agent of the Elector Palatine, an important responsibility because of the strong ties between the elector's court and the English government.

On one occasion, in 1645, Harrington was able, in the midst of the deteriorating political situation, to gain an appropriation of two thousand pounds to cover the expenses of the elector's family in Holland. By that time the possibility of the elector's restoration in Bohemia was rather slim, and this success, given the circumstances surrounding it, is significant. Harrington may have helped the elector's cause by his decision to support Parliament against the king, even to the extent of collecting money in Lincolnshire for the parliamentary cause. Most accounts place Harrington outside, or above, most of the political storms that were just beginning to gather: "James of Sapcote sat speculating about the form such a government should take [a government that would deliver England from its plight], in 'a versatile timber house' off Birdcage Walk in London."

This period of reflection and relative inactivity was probably not completely satisfying for Harrington after a life of involvement in politics. Curious and concerned, he left his study to attend (1646) the parliamentary commissioners when they brought Charles from Newcastle to a place nearer London. The king, who had gone north once more, had been captured by his Scottish enemies, who had then given him to his parliamentary enemies in return for money. Harrington's presence during this journey was noted by both the parliamentary commissioners and by those loyal courtiers who remained with King Charles. His position on the political questions was close to that of the Parliament, but he was a friend of King Charles and had been in his service. For this reason, he was trusted and well regarded by both sides; and, as a result, he became one of four gentlemen agreed upon by king and commissioners to serve as grooms of the royal bedchamber during this period of the king's arrest.

This appointment and his reputation for honesty and evenhandedness placed Harrington at the center of the continuing negotiations between King Charles and his adversaries. He talked often with people of all factions, he apparently worked hard to find some ground for agreement, and he spoke with the king about the virtues and the necessity of a commonwealth: "They had often discourses concerning government but when they hapned to talk of a commonwealth, the King seemed not to endure it."[11] This attitude of Charles' was half of the problem that Harrington and the other peacemakers faced. The other half was the narrow-mindedness and meanness of the "presbyterian divines" who stood behind the Parliament and urged it on. These men could see little good in the king and his family; and, when Harrington warned them that a settlement depended upon some moderation of their demands concerning reorganization of the established church, they began to suspect his intentions and honesty. The gradual deterioration of the relations between the king and Parliament paralleled the loss in confidence, on the part of the parliamentary faction, that Harrington was undergoing.

Harrington, in his conversations with King Charles, had slowly been convinced that much of what was being charged against the monarch was ill-founded, and "he became passionately affected with him, and took all occasions to vindicate him in what company soever he hapned to be." Later, when the king was being moved from Holdenby to Hampton Court, and then began the travels that ended finally in his execution, Harrington's defense became so bold that he was told that he could no longer wait upon the king. In the later stages of the king's journey, Harrington was allowed to travel in the royal coach; but, when he was asked to take an oath that he would not help the king escape, Harrington refused and was placed under arrest. Major General Ireton, a prominent officer in the parliamentary army, gained his release.

During the time that the king was held at the Palace of St. James, Harrington visited him; and, when the trial was over and the king condemned, Harrington accompanied him to the scaffold, "where, a little before, he receiv'd a token of his majesty's affection."[12] He later told his friend John Aubrey that he was so distressed by the sight of the execution that he "contracted a disease by it." At age thirty-seven, having seen much, he retired once more to his house near Bird Cage Walk. In his grief, he first turned to poetry and tried his hand at translating Virgil's *Eclogues* and at composing other verse. "Harry Nevill an ingenious and well bred gentleman, and a good (but conceited) poet being his familiar and confident friend, dissuaded him from tampring with poetry. . . ."[13] In the words of John Aubrey, " . . . his Muse was rough." Nevill convinced him, instead, to turn his attention to politics and commonwealths.

Harrington himself says that the writing of *The Commonwealth of Oceana* took two years. Others report that perhaps twenty years went into the reading and research upon which it is based. It is, without doubt, a large book, the product of a meticulous, as well as an imaginative, intelligence and the work of a lifetime. The book was finished late in 1656; and Harrington, convinced that he had found the natural causes that produce the necessary effect of government, set about getting his work published without running afoul of the strict censorship rules that were drawn up and enforced by the government of Oliver Cromwell, the lord protector. The attempted circumvention—dividing the text among three different printers so that the odds favored that one- or two-thirds of the book would escape the censors that were checking all the shops—failed; and the entire text was impounded. After Harrington's first efforts to secure its release were unsuccessful, he turned to Cromwell's daughter, Lady Claypole, who had a record of successful intervention with her father on behalf of "unhappy" people. The story of how Lady Claypole's help was accomplished is a charming one that provides us with some feeling about the wit and style with which his contemporaries always credit Harrington, but which appear too rarely in his writing.

Harrington did not know Lady Claypole, but was admitted to an antechamber to wait for her decision about his request for an audience. While he was waiting, several of her ladies and her three year old daughter came through the room; the daughter, in the immemorial manner of three year olds, was curious about the man; and, when he entertained her, she asked him to pick her up. Harrington obliged; and, when Lady Claypole entered the room to see who it was that had asked to see her, he put the child down on the floor at her feet and said, "Madam, 'tis well you are come at this nick of time, or I had certainly stolen this pretty little lady."[14] "Stolen her," said the mother, "Pray, what to do with her? For she is yet too young to becom your mistress." Harrington replied: "Madam, tho her charms assure her of a more considerable conquest, yet I must confess it is not love but revenge that promted me to commit this theft." "Lord," said Lady Claypole, "What injury have I don you that you should steal my child?" "None at all," replied Harrington, "But that you might be induc'd to prevail with your father to do me justice, by restoring my child that he has stolen."

When the lady said that her father, who had an adequate number of children, would not do such a thing, Harrington explained that it was the "issue of his brain" that had been seized at the printers and held. He gave assurances that the book was harmless, a political romance, and that it was not in the least critical of Oliver Cromwell. She was promised that she would receive one of the first copies of the book when it was off the presses, and Harrington also asked her to tell her father that he intended to dedicate the book to him. Afterward Lady Claypole intervened, Oliver Cromwell relented, and *Oceana* was published. Before Cromwell relented, however, he read the text and observed, a bit sourly it appears, that the gentleman had like to trepan him out of his power, but that what he had by the sword he would not quit for a little paper shot. He said he didn't like government of one man, but that he had become lord protector out of necessity if the peace was to be maintained among various factions. Left to themselves, these factions would never agree to any form of government and would destroy themselves defeating any proposals for solution.

When notice of the publication of *The Commonwealth of Oceana* appeared in the *Stationers' Register* of September 19, 1656, the announcement called attention to the dedication to the lord protector. With this literary effort completed, Harrington was ready to leave his study in the "versatile timber house" in order to plunge into the political world he had left eight years earlier. Cromwell had only two years to live. After his death, the protectorate would stumble on for another eighteen months before Charles II would return from France to reclaim his father's throne. These three and one-half years were lived with passionate intensity by Harrington, and he had little time for study and reflection in his life of action. The process by which his ideas were formed was complete when he went to see Lady Claypole; and, after he emerged from his trouble with Cromwell, he began a career of advocacy—one of working steadily to realize a commonwealth based upon the principle of the balance.

III   *Harrington's Experience in Perspective*

From this review of his life prior to the publication of *Oceana*, we may draw several conclusions about Harrington. We know, for instance, that his ideas were not produced from what might be considered the experience of being a stranger in a strange land; for the observations he made were not aided or hindered by seeing England and its political customs through eyes that were surprised at the novelty of what they saw. Nor is the question of class necessarily germane to the context of Harrington's ideas and observations; for rich or poor, rising or falling, he and the Harringtons had been at home in England and usually had ready, direct or indirect, access to the sources of power. If James Harrington was moved to think and write out of unhappiness with his own, or his family's, position in England's politics, we find it difficult to see what produced this dissatisfaction. He had been, after all, a valued friend of King Charles, perhaps even his confidant for a while; and he had dear friends occupying important positions in Parliament.

During the period of Cromwell's supremacy, when Harrington had withdrawn from politics and when his influence or access to power was limited, the class with which Harrington is most closely associated by historians, the lesser gentry either rising or falling, was firmly in the saddle; and this might have been, if his association with them was as close as thought, reason for his satisfaction; but such was not the case. Despite the justified assumption of many scholars that *Oceana* was written to refute Hobbes, to assert a Machiavellian commonwealth, or to propose a means of deliverance for an unhappy land, it is possible to argue that Harrington was more immediately concerned with the evils and faults of Cromwell's Instrument of Government and with the deviations from republican forms found in both the theory and practice of the protectorate. Others have contended that the book was intended as friendly advice to Cromwell—an attempt to persuade him to adjust his government to suit the balance. In either case, Harrington clearly argued in behalf of a principle rather than a class, and he was more interested in remedies than in a particular distribution of power. [15]

We may also note a parallel between Harrington's life and that of Machiavelli in the alternation of political involvement with withdrawal and study. Harrington, who knew about politics from both sides, seems to have been at all times dissatisfied with either one or the other. The first period of withdrawal came at the outbreak of the civil war, the occasion of general dissatisfaction with English politics; and it lasted until Harrington accompanied the parliamentary commissioners to return Charles from Scotland. Perhaps this involvement was due to curiosity, as his biographers have said; it may have been because of boredom. There is also a strong possibility that Harrington, whose life may be seen as an attempt to embody what Machiavelli called *virtu*, realized that, in the face of the destruction of the established order in England, withdrawal contributed little to the common good. There are indications that Harrington resumed politics because of pity for the plight of his friend Charles as well as for that of his country.

The second withdrawal appears to have been a reaction to the execution of Charles, an event that every biographer believes affected Harrington profoundly. All accounts describe his grief in moving and believable terms. Harrington himself said he was made sick by it, and we may believe that he meant this condition to be both mental and physical. Certainly he was absent from public politics for eight years, during which time he mended himself with philosophy, political theory, literature, and friendships. Again, as before, the private life began to pall, and the public life regained its allure.

Harrington, as a man, seems to have been incomplete in either public or private life and moved from one to the other to find a unity in his own life.

Harrington's experiences all exhibit a curious balance in their association of opposites. He was firmly rooted in seventeenth century England; his family was involved in the history of England; but he traveled widely and for a comparatively long time in Europe, immersing himself in the examination of different institutions and histories. We have already noted his ambivalent attitude toward public and private life and the realms of action and thought. Like many other Englishmen of his association, he was part of the royal court in London and of that class of landowner that was called "country" to denote its provinciality and its general opposition to the court.[16] This last association may in part explain why Harrington, for a brief while, could be accepted both by Parliament, dominated in the 1640s by the "country," and by the royalists in the king's court. Harrington divided not just his time between Rand, his father's home in the country, and his own house in London, but also his loyalty between the parliamentary cause and the king's own person. He was a useful man when the wood was green and hope abounded, but he was easily cast aside when the wood was dry and the fires of conflict were burning.

In this association of opposites we can find the keys to unlock the origin of the balance. We may recall, at this point, the chief characteristics of this principle and its centrality in Harrington's thought. That power depends upon wealth and does so out of necessity is a principle based upon observation; and, universal in its application, it applies to relationships between individuals, to those within institutions, and to those between groups of people. In the England of his time, Harrington need not have lived long nor traveled far from his father's home to discover grounds for this statement—or for his emphasis upon land as the preeminent form of wealth. Rand, Sir Sapcote Harrington's home, was in Lincolnshire; in that shire, during the decade of 1621 - 1631, there were five bad harvest years; and it was reported that for many of the landless and unemployed poor, "Dogg's flesh is a dainty disch, and the other day one stole a scheepe, whoe for meere hunger tore a legge out, and didd eat itt raw."[17]

These adverse conditions existed during the same time in the shires of Hertfordshire, Hampshire, Cumberland, and Cornwall. Social historians have called into question the widely held view, both today and in Harrington's time, that the peasants starved to death. The first challenge was lodged, not by a modern social historian, but by a contemporary of Harrington's, John Graunt, who studied burial records in London for the twenty year period 1641 - 1661 and concluded that starvation was very rare even in that great city with many paupers. More recent examinations of registries in countryside parishes indicate that, while starvation was seldom listed as the cause of death in Harrington's time, mortality rates climbed during years with poor harvests; and, though many other maladies were cited, the increase in the death rate may be attributed to malnutrition and to the debilitating effect it had on resistance to disease. Miscarriages increased, the number of beggars grew as the poor began to move from place to place in order to find better conditions or more charitable folk, and infant mortality climbed during these same periods.

We may say that, though the evidence as to whether people actually starved is not absolutely certain, there is a correlation between bad harvests, food shortages, and increased mortality rates; and, not surprisingly, the people in England drew the obvious conclusion. They were hungry enough at times to see starvation as a clear and present danger; writers wrote about it; and public officials went to extraordinary lengths to insure that adequate supplies of food were stored against hard times. While admitting that more investigating must be done in order to be precise about the extent of starvation in Stuart England, one social historian, Peter Laslett, concluded that, "No sharper clash of interest, material, economic or even biological, can be easily imagined than that between those with and those without access to the land. In an agrarian economy, at times not far removed from the subsistence level in some areas, this might have meant that when harvests were bad some men could count on surviving, whilst others, the landless could not be so sure."[18] In a small village, even the young son of a knight could not have been shielded from the brutal reality of a series of poor harvests. One of Harrington's early experiences could reasonably have been of the singular importance of land as the producer of food.

Harrington's early life served in other ways as a basis for the principle of the balance. The social structure of small villages and the families that lived in them remained, to a significant degree, essentially patriarchal. Masters were to servants as fathers were to children, and the oldest (or older) sons were to their siblings what princes were to subjects. As the first born son of a well-to-do knight living in a very small village, Harrington lived in a comfortable patriarchal world in which the heads of families stood over everyone else and where, among the heads of families, those with land stood in the first rank. The gentry of England, because of this reliance on land, were not at this time concentrated in one or several major places but were more or less scattered on the land throughout all of England, Scotland, and Ireland. Even in good times, those without land were bound to those who had it. If they were not bound by the proximate danger of starvation, they were bound by its remote danger; and this dependency was reinforced by custom, habit, and even law.

When Harrington left Rand and attended the university, or when he returned from his travels and entered the king's service as a member of the privy council, he probably found little to undermine the validity of his early experience concerning the importance of land in the English scheme of things. The men from the nobility and gentry at Oxford all came from families that owned land. The continuing debate or controversy over the rise or fall of the lesser gentry centers upon an application Harrington made of his principle to analyze the contemporary situation in England and not of the relation of power to land or wealth. H. R. Trevor-Roper, in his telling criticism of Harrington, attacks both Harrington's principle and his analysis; and he makes a persuasive case that gaining office at court was the means by which men increased their power and prestige, not by acquiring more land. This contention presents some problems, but it also provides a means for defending the principle of the balance, as Harrington defines it, against the criticisms.

In Stuart England, there were offices and there were offices. Some of these could make a man's fortune and reputation, and others could ruin him. Harrington's own family offers an excellent example of the second category.[19] His granduncle, Baron John Harrington of Exton, was visited with several offices and honors by his sovereign, James I. He was, as noted, appointed guardian to the Princess Elizabeth and made responsible for her upkeep and education. Elizabeth was a charming but spoiled and extravagant young woman, and the office was an expensive one. Since Baron Harrington was quite wealthy in land and in money and goods, he could have sustained this considerable drain on his resources. However, James I also awarded him with an embassy abroad, an honor so expensive that other men went to extreme lengths to appear unworthy of such recognition.

The baron had, however, another burden: James' decision to pay

Sir John a royal visit. Not only was the king to be accommodated, but also the entire court and government; and the king and his court traveled and lived on a lavish scale. To pare royal expenses is the reason that royal visits were paid. Sir John's brother, Sir Henry Harrington of Elmesthorpe, took up a military career and was given the honor and office of leading an expedition in Ireland against Tyrone's rebels. The result of this was a "positively disgraceful encounter" and great deal of financial outlay. Such honors and offices required subsidies, and both Sir Henry and Sir John borrowed in order to support their activities. Unlike others favored by the king, such as Sir Julius Caesar, who realized twenty-two hundred pounds a year as master of the rolls, and Sir Roger Wilbraham, the solicitor general of Ireland, who was able to leave his three daughters four thousand pounds per year in his will out of his profits of honor, these two Harrington brothers and their families sank, heavily encumbered with debt, into political obscurity. The third brother, Sir James Harrington of Ridlington, James Harrington's grandfather, alone escaped honor, office, and their reward and remained solvent. The problem with using office as an indication of a rising career in politics is the numerous examples of men who ruined themselves by gaining more distinction than they could afford. Most offices were purchased by their holders for the price of several years' income. What happened to a man's fortune once ensconced in office depended upon his ability to maintain a gentleman's establishment or "port" that was in proportion to what he gained from the prudent management of his post. It was not a simple calculation, and mistakes were destructive.

What happened to the holdings of those who failed is what makes the validity of Harrington's theory more certain. The failures borrowed first against their income and then against their landed property. When they defaulted, they lost their land. With regularity the holders of these notes fell into two categories. There were, first of all, an increasing number of successful merchants and officeholders in London who were drawn to investments in such notes; and the reason for their interest was unique to England among European countries at that time. These merchants, who were the unlanded sons, in many instances, of the gentry that remained in the country, measured their success by their ability to drop or disassociate themselves from the commercial or mercantile trades in the cities and to return to the world of their childhoods—that of the landed gentry. This mobility was, in a real way, both geographic and social. Sons without an inheritance—and in an England governed by the custom of primogeniture there were always many—went into the professions, into the military, or to the city and trade to make their living and then "retired to the countryside as soon as opportunity presented itself." "Londoners who happened to inherit country houses nearly always seem to have taken up their residence there and left the city." [20]

The other group of men who invested in mortgages were those officeholders who were able to make the delicate calculation described above. Their estates grew in number and size, and they took advantage not only of those who ruined themselves in politics but also those who could not improve their position on the land by increasing their rents or their crop yields.

All of this exchange of place has been mustered as support for the observation that in England land was the touchstone of wealth in the seventeenth century. It could and did serve as the basis for gaining power and position as it surely did in the case of the nobility and most of the gentry. This corresponds with major parts of Harrington's thesis. It is also clear that those with power used the income that came from power to purchase land and more land. So far as both cases are concerned, there is no real contradiction with Harrington's balance. The determinism of Harrington's balance, we must remember, is mitigated by its reversibility: either those with land will gain power over those without it or those with power will use it to dispossess those who have land in order to maintain power. Both cases are covered by the rule and, given Harrington's education and political experience, familiar to him. We will deal with the more specific analysis of England and with the rise of the gentry made by Harrington in applying the balance.

Harrington's experience in both London and the country presented him with evidence of land's importance, but he was impressed in Europe by what he might never have noticed in England. As we have observed, his reading and his observations in Venice could not have supported a concept of balance based upon land alone. In Holland and Venice, which he knew first hand, power grew out of money and goods, which grew, in turn, out of trade. He could imagine "antique" societies in which there was no private landed property because he had read about such. Thus, in its most complete form, the balance encompasses Harrington's experiences in Europe as well as in England and unifies them in the relationship of power to wealth. This improvement was, to an extent, forced out of Harrington by his critics, but it does indicate that he could call upon his observations on the Continent to serve his purposes as a theorist and polemicist.

The traveler and the stranger do not see everything that may be important, though they may take note of the things that are interesting. One problem in journalism, and in the tradition of the grand tour, is the often noticed incongruity between what is interesting, either novel or quaint, and what is important. In "passing through," most of us are more taken with the colorful and picturesque aspects of a strange land. At home, the familiarity of what appears interesting to strangers, and the ubiquitous, and usually unnoticed, regularities of each day, develop into a way of life and a sense of what is important.

This sense is not always spoken, but an appreciation of it can be found in the following statement of J. G. A. Pocock about what Harrington sensed at home but could not have noticed in Europe. "One of many reasons that land, not trade, is the necessary background of Harrington's thought—why he is unable to give a convincing account of how master-servant relationships determine the distribution of power in Holland or even Venice—is that his ideas hinge so greatly on the contrast between an England in which the ordinary proprietor was the military tenant of a feudal magnate and one in which he is free to bear arms in his own or the commonalty's quarrel."[21] This view of Harrington's balance has him equating the ownership of land with liberty, or at least the freedom on the part of the landowner to choose in which disputes he wishes to become embroiled.

Nevertheless, Harrington is at his weakest in regard to the balance when he moves beyond England and makes an attempt to establish its validity in reference to contemporary Holland and Venice. Because of this he has less success in showing the universality of the balance. Ironically, though Harrington's experiences abroad initially led him to develop an interest in politics and history, and add a dimension to his thought that is ordinarily lacking in that of most of his contemporaries, these experiences were less than adequate to support his claim to universality.

Felix Rabb has written concerning the balance, ". . . certainly there was enough in Harrington's experience to enable him to deduce such a principle from it." These experiences, both first and second hand, are many and various; they contain elements of oppositeness; but in many ways they complete and support one another. In every age, much evidence indicates that power and dominion must be considered first in political theory; and, in Harrington's time, with the civil war in England and the Thirty Years War in Europe, this consideration may have seemed to be not only the first but the only one. But, even when politics is reduced to the fact of power alone, there are questions to be asked; for only the simple minded are satisfied with an equation that links power to military force. Most observers are astute enough to see that armies and navies are not self-supporting; and it is clear today, with the tax levies in every great nation-state, that power is expensive whether it is being used or only maintained in readiness for use.

To James Harrington, who loaned money to his government to help pay for military adventures in Ireland, and who went among his friends and neighbors in Lincolnshire to raise money for the parliamentary forces, the expense of power *qua* military operations was also clear. This firsthand experience and the secondhand experience that he gained from the books of other writers led him to say ". . . that Riches are Power is (as antient as the first book of THUCYDIDES, or the Politics of ARISTOTLE, and) not omitted by Mr. HOBBS, or any other Politician."[22] With this equation we have returned to Harrington's first principle, except that we have now seen why "Riches" for Harrington were more closely linked to land than to money or goods. For land, in the medieval context, was the origin of obligation; and this obligation, owed by the worker of the land to the owner of it, made the medieval army possible. The same land, with the medieval system of obligations removed, still served as the source of food and money to support the armies of the emerging modern age.

Political theorists set themselves the task of discovering, and even building, unity in the realms of political activity and political thought. Earlier we said that they are moved by some perception or experience of trouble in the world to unite the precinct, the university, and the church. A first step in this effort is their discovery in their own experience of the world and with other people of a corresponding unity; and this unity is the foundation upon which the more ambitious structures will be built. The principle of the balance, though it served Harrington well in the construction of the ideal commonwealth and in his analysis of the world's troubles, served first as a means of organizing and unifying his own experiences.

CHAPTER 3

Of Republics and Commonwealths

I   *The Best Form of Government*

IN keeping with the custom of authors everywhere, James Harrington provided his relatives with copies of his *Oceana* when it was printed. And his relatives, in the usual manner, circulated the books among their friends. One of Harrington's sisters, Lady Ashton, presented a copy to H. Ferne D.D., mentioned earlier as a critic of *Oceana*, as a mark of respect and with a request that he give her his judgment of the book; and Ferne's letter of thanks, dated November 4, 1656, to her ladyship, first provoked Harrington to defend his ideas. There would be other critics, and some of them much more able than Dr. Ferne, but his short letter of "censure" was the opening shot and his targets were well chosen:

I received a book directed to me from your ladyship with the intimation I should express my sense of it. . . . Give me leave then, Madame, in plain English to say, that albeit the author hath shewn good sufficiency of parts, and taken much pains in order to his design; yet I conceive, first, that he is not a little mistaken in thinking the Israel commonwealth or government under Moses so appliable unto his purpose as he would make it. Next, that when the question 'twixt his form [the commonwealth] and the monarchical is disputed over and over again, reason and experience will still plead for the latter. Nor can the balance he pretends stands so steady in his form, as in a well tempered monarchy, by reason the temptation of advancing are more likely to sway with many in a commonwealth, than with one, etc. in the height of dignity. Next, when I consider such a change by this model from what was ever in, etc. and that the agrarian, with some other levelling orders, are the laws of it, I should think the nature of men was first to be new model'd, before they would be capable of this.[1]

Every statement in this letter provoked Harrington; for, though the theory of the balance was left untouched by this volley, almost everything else that Harrington held to be important was hit. For Ferne, a cleric and a Monarchist, a monarchy was more stable because it was in keeping with his concept of human nature. Harrington's *Oceana* contained profoundly anticlerical and antimonarchical sentiments, all justified on the basis of the Bible, reason, experience, political theory, and common sense. Harrington replied to the doctor on all counts, but the greatest part of his response concerned the value and benefit of the commonwealth, the best form of government. This idea was, with him, second in importance only to the balance; and, though his admiration of commonwealths was not original, his justification of that form of government was.

Harrington established the link between the balance and commonwealths in "Preliminaries I" of *Oceana*. "Preliminaries II" of the same work makes specific application of the balance and the form of the commonwealth to conditions in England. It was Harrington's method to establish the validity of his principles in terms of both abstract and concrete frames of reference. Although Dr. Ferne's brief criticism was restricted to the theoretical argument about the superiority of the commonwealth, later critics enlarged the attack to include the suitability of that form of government for England.

Harrington is convinced that the commonwealth is the best form of government on several points that at first seem incompatible. It is best whenever it is based upon a balance that rests in the hands of many propertyowners, rather than a few or only one. Another form of government under such circumstances would be a perversion of its form and of short duration. Even of the good forms, the commonwealth is best in the sense that it is in accord with human nature. If Harrington had been an economic determinist of the rigid sort, he would not have had to make his case in terms of human nature, as well as in terms of the balance. When it is clear to his readers that, no matter what the balance is at a given time, those in power can prevail against it and alter it to fit the form of government they desire, Harrington must show that, if the balance supports a commonwealth, good reasons exist for not allowing a tyrant to become a king or an oligarchy to become an aristocracy by using force to change the balance.

Under these circumstances, the question, "Why should there be a commonwealth?" cannot be answered by saying that it fits the balance. To provide an acceptable answer, Harrington had to go farther and link the empirical association of property and power with the normative association of law and the common interest. He needed to show that force, which is the basis for all good governments in the theory of the balance, is not only different from violence, the basis for all perverted forms of government, but will vary from little in a commonwealth to more and much more in monarchies and aristocracies. The defense and the justification of the commonwealth, then, are made on both empirical and normative grounds. Harrington was able, in this particular attempt at unity, to convince himself, if not all his readers, that the traditional tension between the good and the expedient had been resolved.

Harrington poses the essential duality of the problem early in the "Preliminaries": ". . . the principles of government are twofold; internal, or the goods of the mind; and external, or the goods of fortune. The goods of the mind are natural or acquir'd virtues, as wisdom, prudence and courage, etc. The goods of fortune are riches. . . . To the goods of the mind answers authority; to the goods of fortune, power or empire."[2] After this statement, the emphasis is placed upon power and empire, for the distinction made between authority and power, the difference between choice and necessity, places a premium on power and necessity. But Harrington does return to pose a related problem; the discrepancy between goods of fortune and goods of the mind is not merely one of definition; it has important and unfortunate effects upon politics and government.

The great hope of political philosophers is to unite the goods of fortune and those of mind in one legislator and in one government; and this unity would come closest to what is the greatest work of God. Harrington specifically mentions the philosopher-king of Plato as an example of this unity, and quotes Solomon to the effect that, "Folly is set in great dignity, and the rich sit in low places. I have seen servants upon horses, and princes walking as servants upon the earth."[3] This predicament, in which mankind has ever been, moves Harrington to inspired exhortation:

Sad complaints, that the principles of power and of authority, the goods of mind and of fortune, do not meet and twine in the wreath or crown of empire! Wherfore, if we have anything of piety or of prudence, let us raise ourselves out of the mire of private interest to the contemplation of virtue, and put a hand to the removal of this evil from under the sun; this evil against which no government that is secure must be perfect. . . . We have wander'd the earth to find out the balance of power: but to find out that of authority, we must ascend, as I said, nearer heaven, or to the image of God, which is the soul of man.

For Harrington, and for many who pondered this problem before him, the soul of man is the mistress of two rivals, passion and reason, which continually vie for her attachment. The soul is identified with the will. Attached to passion, the will is the prisoner of error and sin; but, when it operates under the influence of reason, the will is free and is virtue itself in action.

The anthropomorphism that is part of the Western theoretical tradition is embodied in Harrington's explanation of the character of government. Just as Plato said that the city is man writ large, Harrington says that the government is the soul of the city or nation: ". . . wherfore that which was reason in the debate of a commonwealth being brought forth by the result, must be virtue; and for as much as the soul of a city or nation is the soverain power, her virtue must be law. But the government whose law is virtue, is the same whose empire is authority, and whose authority is empire."[4] The identification that Harrington wishes to make becomes clearer when he writes: "Again, if the liberty of a man consists in the empire of his reason, the absence wherof would betray him to the bondage of his passions; then the liberty of a commonwealth consists in the empire of her laws, the absence wherof would betray her to the lust of tyrants."

These statements proved to be those that caused trouble for some of Harrington's readers. Matthew Wren, perhaps the most astute of Harrington's contemporary critics, put it very well: ". . . seeing the whole force of the argument rests upon the similitude of government with the soul of man, we may be instructed what the soul is, and what the whole philosophy belonging to it. And then and not before, will it be the time to consider how far the similitude between that and government will hold true."[5] The same criticism has been made of Plato's anthropomorphism; the validity of the identification cannot be established by the empirical method, but it so frequently appears in philosophy that an outright denial of its reality places critics in the position of cutting political theory and philosophy loose from the moorings of a common experience.

As if anticipating criticism on this point, Harrington immediately cited Aristotle and Titus Livy as authorities for his contention that a commonwealth is an empire of laws and, therefore, of reason and of freedom. This formulation was posed against its opposite—a government of men, of passion, and of subjugation to necessity. In a commonwealth, Harrington says, riches and power and liberty belong to every man. Harrington approaches the freedom that he values from two directions: freedom is, first of all, the product of riches, of land and money or goods; and these riches obviate the ability of others who possess these things to control a man who also has them. These same riches that remove necessity from the door of a man's house and keep it at bay also put their possessor in a position to make choices: he can decide which private or public affairs and which disputes deserve his involvement, and he can choose his friends and his pastimes.

Liberty, or freedom, is also the product of reason or, more precisely, the direction of the soul or will by reason. A man whose life is the subject of reason can also make choices that override or check the influence of passion in his life. Free of the cruel necessity that is the fruit of passion, a man may, by choice, direct his efforts toward what is beautiful and true. The ideal for any man is to combine both the possession of riches and a soul directed by reason in one life. Twice freed from necessity, such a life comes close to that which was intended by God for his creatures. On the level of individual life, this unity is what Harrington seeks for the entire nation.

Unfortunately, despite the anthropomorphic identification, the transfer of this accomplishment from individual to communal life has not been easy for theorists to make; or at least it has not been easy for them to make in a way that convinces us that it has, in fact, been truly made. Reason is the root of freedom and virtue in a man's life, but a commonwealth governed by reason is an empire of laws and not of men. "But seeing that they that make the laws in commonwealths are but men, the main question seems to be, how a commonwealth comes to be an empire of laws, and not of men? or how the debate or result of a commonwealth is so sure to be according to reason; seeing they who debate, and they who resolve, be but men? and as often as reason is against a man, so often will a man be against reason."[6]

The answer to this riddle, so far as Harrington goes, is achieved by another identification, that of reason with interest; for ". . . reason is nothing but interest, there be divers interests, and so divers reasons."[7] What follows from this identification is the construction of a hierarchy of interests or reasons in which we move from the private interest or reason of one man to the interest or reason of the state—of the one, several, or many rulers of the state—but we finally ascend to the ultimate, the interest or reason of all mankind. To establish more firmly the primacy of this last type of reason or interest Harrington again resorts to authority, Richard Hooker, whom he quotes at some length and to somewhat dubious effect:

> Now if we see even in those natural agents that want sense, that as in themselves they have a law which directs them in the means wherby they tend to their own perfection, so likewise that another law there is, which touches them as they are sociable parts united into one body, a law which binds them each to others good, and all to prefer the good of the whole, before whatsoever their own particular, as when stones, or heavy things forsake their ordinary wont or center, and fly upwards, as if they heard themselves commanded to let go the good they privately wish, and to relieve the present distress of nature in common.[8]

What Hooker has in mind are two "goods" or "perfections": one, a creature seeks for its own sake; another, for the sake of all others. The second is more excellent, but Hooker had no illusions about the willingness of humans or others to sacrifice the first in order to attain the second. It was as remarkable for that to happen as for "stones, or heavy things . . . [to] fly upwards," for Hooker was still thinking and writing in a world he perceived to be incapable of the unity at which Harrington aimed.

Harrington summarized this statement of Hooker's: "There is a common right, law of nature, or interest of the whole; which is more excellent, and so acknowledg'd to be by the agents themselves, than the right or interest of the parts only."[9] Hugo Grotius was also cited as having observed that even animals "abstain from their own profit, either in regard of those of the same kind, or at least of their young." Although Hooker and Grotius are agreed that some sacrifice of individual good is necessary to promote the good of others or of the whole, they recognized that the measure of this sacrifice is what has always prevented that good from being fully realized. A man, after all, can acknowledge the superiority or greater excellence of the common right, interest, or good without ever being willing to give up one jot or tittle of what he holds as his own in order to move his community closer to that good. Harrington avoided facing this limitation.

With all of this established to his satisfaction, Harrington moved to cap his argument: ". . . if reason be nothing else but interest, and the interest of mankind be the right interest, then the interest of mankind must be right reason. Now compute well; for if the interest of popular government com the nearest to the interest of mankind, then the reason of popular government must com the nearest to right reason."[10] It is true, we recall, that the reason or interest of state is the reason or interest of the rulers; in a commonwealth, it is the reason or interest of the people who are the rulers. So long as the nation-state is the ultimate political entity, the commonwealth comes closer than any other form of government to the most excellent interest or reason—to that of all mankind. Harrington has thus justified the commonwealth not only in terms of the balance,—that is, that it is best given a certain distribution of property—but also, on an abstract level, that it is most excellent in reference either to the common reason or to the interest of mankind. This second justification is, as yet, incomplete; for Harrington still has to demonstrate how it is possible to take the selfish individual interests of many and mold them into a single common interest.

II   The Empire of Law

Although the interest of the commonwealth is the common interest, and its reason is right reason, the interest of one man and his reason is always his alone. A man will always, according to Harrington, look upon reason only to discover whether it is for him or against him. In a commonwealth, each man must be persuaded, ". . . not to carve himself of that which he desires most, but to be mannerly at the public table, and give the best from himself to decency and the common interest."[11] Harrington believed that he had found a method that would ensure this good behavior. "Known even to girls," it consists in having the proposing of alternatives done by one and the selection of alternatives performed by the other, as in dividing a cake or a piece of fruit. Both have an interest, and each is well served in this method. The person dividing divides equally because, if this is not done, the person selecting will pick the larger or better half and will leave the divider with the lesser. Since the person selecting knows as much as the divider, he is willing to leave the matter as it stands; he is secure in the knowledge that having first choice will keep the divider honest.

Harrington was particularly pleased with this discovery because it was practical and simple and its homeliness probably appealed to a man who was occasionally annoyed by the pomposities of university scholars. There is no mistaking his enthusiasm: "O the depth of the wisdom of God! and yet by the mouths of babes and sucklings has he set forth his strength; that which great philosophers are disputing upon in vain is brought to light by two harmless girls, even the whole mystery of a commonwealth, which lies only in dividing and chusing."

It is possible, also, in any body of men to determine who shall have the natural right of dividing and who shall have the natural right of choosing. In the process of discussing matters, a natural aristocracy will be seen to exist. Some men will speak and more will listen, having deferred to the recognized superiority of the speakers. These few men have the authority of fathers in society; they are not so much the commanders of men as they are advisers. Their responsibility is to debate or, in keeping with the primitive example of Harrington, to divide; and the many, the people, will do the choosing. Every commonwealth, if it desires to overcome the inherent selfishness of man, will be composed of two legislative bodies or councils: a senate to debate, and an assembly to choose. Although the few may be wise enough to see what is right, there is always the matter of interest; and the interest of the few "is not the profit of mankind, nor of a commonwealth." While the few represent the wisdom of the commonwealth, the many represent its interest. The first may be styled an aristocracy; the second is the people. Where there are many people, the assembly should be composed of their representatives. Whatever has been debated by the senate and resolved by the people is enacted out of both authority and power; for "the authority of the fathers and the power of the people," when they concur, make a law.

Once a law is made, it must be enforced or executed; and this function, in a commonwealth, is performed by what Harrington called "the magistracy." In neither art nor nature, said Harrington, can there be a commonwealth without this particular combination of assembly, senate, and magistracy or of democracy, aristocracy, and monarchy. This form of government was admired by Polybius, and Harrington mentioned Machiavelli as a proponent of this mixed form. In addition to these authorities, Harrington provided a survey of other commonwealths to show that each, to some measure and in some form, had these same institutions: an assembly, a senate, a magistracy.

Harrington began his survey with copious citations from the Bible in an attempt to show that Israel was a commonwealth, the case that drew the attention of Dr. Ferne. In quick succession, he also gave short descriptions of the governments of Athens, Sparta, Carthage, Rome, Venice, Switzerland, and Holland for the purpose of showing the uniformity of their structures. He finished by establishing an analogy between the commonwealth of Israel in which God was said to reign as king and all commonwealths governed by law, in which, when the law is king, God is king.

III   Oceana *Contra* Leviathan

To a degree, Harrington's propounding of the balance was a corrective to the looser description, or definition, of power contained in Hobbes' *Leviathan*. Harrington, in developing his justification of the commonwealth, found himself contending with Hobbes, who had questioned the value of the ancient writers who praised commonwealths and who had been critical of that form of government. The problem, Hobbes felt, was caused by the reading of Greek and Latin authors by young men who associated the great deeds performed by heroes with "Their popular form of government, not considering the frequent seditious and civil wars produc'd by the imperfection of their polity."[12] These deeds and the prosperity enjoyed in those times came instead, thought Hobbes, from the influence of "particular men."

Harrington seized upon this last point and argued that this influence had been transmitted because of great virtue, that this virtue had been produced by the best education, that the best education required the best laws, and that only an excellent polity could write the best laws. This response he judged adequate to Hobbes' first complaint, and he proceeded to answer the criticism that many ancient polities had been torn by sedition, civil war, and unrest. He accused Hobbes of criticizing the general form of the commonwealth because some commonwealths had failed to achieve the perfection of the form. Harrington asserted that monarchy, which was the form of government most appealing to Hobbes, even in its perfection contains flaws simply because some men living under a king have an interest and, having the interest, may have the power to engage in seditious activity. Since monarchies must depend upon armies maintained by the king himself or upon the support of a nobility who use their power to maintain the king, this dependency became the source of sedition in monarchies. Ambitious and unscrupulous generals or lords had the interest and the power to topple a king and raise up a new one.

Harrington said, on behalf of commonwealths, more "than Leviathan has said or ever will be able to say for monarchy." No commonwealth, said Harrington, has ever been conquered by a monarchy until it had first destroyed itself from within; but some commonwealths have defeated monarchies. Commonwealths that have been seditious have not been so because of a generic fault but as the result of some particular shortcoming in its own form. Commonwealths that have been what Harrington called "equal" have never been seditious. Finally, "That it is the government, which, attaining to perfect equality, has such a libration in the frame of it, that no man living can shew which way any man or men, in or under it, can contract any such interest or power as should be able to disturb the commonwealth with sedition; wherfore an equal commonwealth is that only which is without flaw, and contains in it the full perfection of government."[13]

With the conclusion of this second criticism and refutation of Hobbes, Harrington provided two additional justifications of the form of the commonwealth. The commonwealth, in Harrington's account, is shown to be superior in military prowess to monarchies; and it is, when it is near the top of its form, more stable and more prosperous than a monarchy because of the bringing together of the elements that might ordinarily serve to pull a community apart. Superstructure and foundation are unified in keeping with the principle of the balance; reason and passion are united under the heading of interest; authority and power come together through debate and resolution in the senate and assembly. Only one question remains, and Harrington raised it in the refutation of Hobbes. Harrington had explained how the private and common interest may be accommodated in the processes and institutions of a commonwealth, but the matter of power still remained. If these processes and institutions were to fail in their goal of preventing the development of seditious interests, what would prevent those so disposed from destroying the balance and altering the form. There is an indication that Harrington has discerned the difference that distinguishes successful from unsuccessful commonwealths. That difference is found in his use of the term "equal commonwealth."

Obviously, equal commonwealths do not become seditious; those that are unequal will ultimately be torn by dissension. The terms refer to the access to, or the possession of, power, and the problem that Harrington next proposed to solve was how the foundation and superstructure of a commonwealth could be kept secure against chance.

IV   The Division of Commonwealths

Only a commonwealth in the perfection of its form is proof against the changes that produce dissension. There are two sources of power in any state; one adheres in the superstructure, the other in the foundation. The power of the foundation was viewed as natural by Harrington, and the power in the superstructure was considered artificial. One was natural force; the other was unnatural force or violence if used to alter the balance; but changes in either could endanger the perfect commonwealth.

Harrington was aware, after his reading of Machiavelli, that other studies of commonwealths had made distinctions among various specimens. Commonwealths that were "single" were composed of only one group of people such as biblical Israel, Athens, and Sparta; and those that were "leagues" or associated groups of people were represented by Switzerland and Holland with their various provinces and their different languages and dialects. To Machiavelli, who based his typology of commonwealths on the criterion of foreign policy, there were commonwealths for "preservation" and ones for "increase"; and this differentiation took cognizance of the goals and ambitions of the nation in regard to its neighbors and to the world in general. Those nations bent upon winning an empire were commonwealths for "increase" and required a large number of citizens in order to achieve their objectives. Nations satisfied with their wealth and territory, for whatever reason, were commonwealths for "preservation," their needs could be scaled down, and only a number of citizens sufficient for the defense of the state were required. This classification, very similar to the contemporary division of nations into status quo and revisionist, was particularly useful for the political context in which Machiavelli lived and worked. The city-state system in sixteenth century Italy required such an analytical tool in order to make sense of the policies and goals of the shifting alliances that competed for advantage.

Harrington was responding to a different environment and to different demands when he established "equal" and "unequal" categories of commonwealth. In the "Preliminaries," he claimed that his typology had not been noted in the previous works on commonwealths and that his difference between equal and unequal ". . . is the main point, especially as to domestic peace and tranquility; for to make a commonwealth inequal, is to divide it into partys, which sets them at perpetual varience, the one party endeavoring to preserve their eminence and inequality, and the other to attain to equality."[14] To Harrington, this fault in the body politic had caused perpetual strife in Rome between the people and the nobility who sat in the senate. This strife, when it was joined by other problems, produced the decline of the Roman Republic. Although Machiavelli had been so impressed by this phenomenon that he was convinced that such strife was unavoidable and even believed that it was healthy, Harrington could not be so sanguine. He had lived through a bloody and traumatic period of factional strife; and, as he wrote *Oceana*, he was very much aware that the great impediment to a peaceful resolution of England's constitutional crisis was the continued existence of such factions as those complained of by Cromwell. Harrington was convinced, therefore, that this internal disorder must be ended; and he was convinced by what he knew of the Venetian commonwealth that it could be ended.

Such an "equal" commonwealth would be equal in both the balance or foundation and in the superstructure, and the constitutional devices for achieving such equality were the "Agrarian Law" and "Rotation." The first applied to the limitation of property; the second, to a limitation on the holding of office. Harrington's definition of the "Agrarian Law" is "A perpetual law establishing and preserving the balance of dominion by such a distribution, that no one man or number of men, within the compass of a few or aristocracy, can come to over power the whole people by their possession in lands."[15] This law, if enforced, would eliminate the possibility that those holding power in the superstructure could or would reverse the natural relationship between the balance and the government.

The problem of enforcing the Agrarian consistently and equitably was to be solved by rotation in office: "Equal rotation is equal vicissitude in government, or succession to magistracy confer'd for such convenient terms, enjoying equal vacations, as take in the

whole body by parts, succeeding others, thro the free election or
suffrage of the people." To prolong the time that men could serve
as magistrates would make it possible for their own interests to overcome their generous instincts. Moreover, the power that would ac-
crue to those who benefited from such prolongation would serve to
overcome the effect of the Agrarian . Since that law might be safely
ignored by one secure in office, the foundation might be subverted
through the superstructure: "The contrary [to rotation] wher unto is
prolongation of magistracy, which, trashing the wheel of rotation,
destroys the life or natural motion of a commonwealth."

A third device, the ballot, was also proposed by Harrington in
order to prevent private interest from displacing the public interest.
Such a procedure would only be successful, however, when the
private interest could be freely expressed and not hindered by
promises, obligations, fear, shyness, or any other emotional obstacle
to free expression. Harrington admitted that his idea of the ballot
was drawn generally from Cicero's description of the method used
by the people of Rome, but more especially from the example set by
the republic of Venice. Voting by ballot was to be done secretly to
protect the freedom of the voter and to preserve the vote from the
outside interests mentioned above. The ballot consisted of two
pieces of wood or two balls of different colors to signify negative or
affirmative votes. The voter, who was to be given one of each color,
was to cast one and discard the other. The interest of the people was
no more or less, given this process, than the vote of the majority. By
common agreement, however, the result of the votes would be
taken as constituting the common interest or reason, an expression
of the common will.

Following this brief survey and description of the general institutional structure and balloting processes found in an equal commonwealth, Harrington was ready to essay a complete definition of
the ideal form: "An equal commonwealth (by that which has bin
said) is a government establish'd upon an equal Agrarian, arising
into the superstructures or three orders, the senate deliberating and
proposing, the people resolving, and the magistracy executing by an
equal rotation thro the suffrage of the people given by the ballot." [16]
This commonwealth is, in a sense, laid up in the heavens; thus far it
is an ideal commonwealth composed of bits and pieces taken from
different writers and regimes.

Harrington anticipated the question that is as old as Plato's
Republic: "Can such a state ever exist?" An approximation of such

a commonwealth did exist in experience, according to Harrington. Venice was a commonwealth for preservation, but it was not perfectly equal. It was, among others existing or having existed, however, the most nearly perfect commonwealth. To Harrington, it was important to demonstrate, in circumstances that demanded concrete solutions to serious problems, that the ideal commonwealth was not a hopeless goal. Venice, as described by Harrington, was the proof that the equal commonwealth was not beyond the reach of human beings. If the equal commonwealth could be built, the unity Harrington sought would rise with it.

The goal of political theory had been that philosophers be kings and kings be philosophers or that princes ride and beggars walk. Harrington began by quoting Plato and Solomon to the effect that deliverance from the incommodities of human existence consisted in finding a way to unite authority and power in the leaders of the state. The equal commonwealth would achieve this unity without putting the philosophers in power. Harrington answered those who argue that even in an equal commonwealth a small elite will rise to the top by saying that these few will be Plato's philosopher-kings, but he was quick to show that they will have authority, not power or empire. The commonwealth is a chariot to which these men are hitched—authority pulling empire—but none of these men will remain in the traces for long since the rotation of the officeholders will remove them at intervals.

This argument is plausible; but Harrington's commonwealth places no special confidence in any limited class of men: its government is to be one of laws and not of men. Authority and power will not be brought together in the philosopher-kings as in Plato's *Republic*; they will be joined in the law, institutions, and processes of the equal commonwealth. This solution bears great similarity to that proposed by Plato in his *Laws*, which contains a description of the second best state. If men, or a majority of men, are not able to transcend their own selfish interests to discover those of the entire community, some abstract entity must be constructed to perform this function. This entity may be the law, or it may be the artificial person described by Hobbes in *Leviathan.*

There are other problems that commonwealths must face. Machiavelli, whom Harrington much admired as a commonwealthsman, had stated two of them (mentioned earlier in reference to the balance and in this chapter) in his discussion of class conflict and of the general uselessness and danger of the gentry to any commonwealth. When Harrington attacked Machiavelli on both points, he asserted in regard to the contributions of the gentry that, whenever commonwealths had been instituted by a man, that man had been a member of the gentry. An impressive list of such worthies—including Moses, Theseus, Solon, Lycurgus, Romulus, Numa, Brutus, Publicola, and the Gracchi—was adduced as evidence that this was the case. Gentlemen had led the armies of the commonwealths; and, where there had not been enough gentlemen, the states had imported them from other lands to serve these purposes. "For where there is not a nobility to hearten the people, they are slothful, regardless of the world, and of the public interest of liberty . . . wherfore let the people embrace the gentry in peace, as the light of their eys; and in war, as the trophy of their arms . . . let the nobility love and cherish the people that afford them a throne much higher in a commonwealth in the acknowledgement of their virtue, than the crowns of monarchs."[17] This acclaim and amity is possible in an equal commonwealth, and Machiavelli's "pernicious error" in regard to the gentry resulted from his failure to understand the principle of the balance and then to be unaware of the difference between equal and unequal commonwealths. The inequality of a commonwealth lies either in a faulty agrarian law—one that perpetuates inequality or fails to protect against inequality—or no agrarian law at all. An additional cause of inequality is the lack of some provision for adequate rotation in office. In extreme cases, an unequal commonwealth may be plagued by a mixture of several of the inadequacies mentioned above. Whenever such a situation exists, creative cooperation between gentry and people is impossible. The great commonwealths of the past faced such difficulties: Athens and Rome had faulty agrarians; Israel and Sparta had irregular rotation in office. Domestic unrest resulted.

A second class of problems that haunt commonwealths concerned religion, or church-state relationships. Harrington began his discussion of this problem by referring to the precedent regarding laws of religion in ancient commonwealths, which were the responsibility of the magistrate. One of the great errors of modern times, according to Harrington, was the usurpation of this power by the papacy. This criticism is reminiscent of that of Marsilio of Padua who saw, in this development, the roots of irreconcilable conflict in the state. Popes and emperors were constantly at odds over a variety of issues. When no resolution to the struggle could be found at the summit of these two great organizations, church and state, a competition inevitably developed between the two sovereigns for the loyalty and support of the people. Interdict and proscription, excommunication and persecution left the people confused and sullen at best and excited them at the worst to violent revolt and to destruction.

Marsilio resolved this dispute in favor of his master, the Holy Roman Emperor; but Harrington's solution was more sophisticated. For his time, when religious disagreements and suspicions were acknowledged by most to be intimately connected with the bloodshed in Europe and England, his formulation must have seemed hopelessly out of touch with reality. Any government, he believed, that pretended to liberty could not suppress liberty of conscience without being guilty of inconsistency. This assertion is balanced by another that labels absurd the desire of an individual man to suppress the liberty of the national conscience. Even in matters of religion, a distinction must exist between the private religious interest of one man and the common religious interest of all. Liberty of conscience for all would make it possible, Harrington argued, for private religion and public religion to stand together.

This possibility is once more demonstrated by reference to the practice in ancient commonwealths. In Israel, where ecclesiastical and civil law were the same, the Sanhedrin, or what Harrington considered the equivalent to a senate in other commonwealths, had control over both. The national religion was the responsibility of this group, but other prophets were granted liberty of conscience. This liberty was not restricted until the commonwealth of Israel had been conquered by the Roman Empire and its processes subverted by Herod, Pilate, and Tiberius. Moreover, Athens and Rome had followed the same pattern in handling the problems of religion. Since then, however, the problem had been handled differently: men had been forced to believe as others believe. Be they bishops, presbyters, or priests, these others had claimed too much when they had forced their religion on others.

Since the nature of religion, says Harrington, does not admit of sensible demonstration, this coercion, he believes, is at the root of war: ". . . wheras the Christian religion is the farthest of any from countenancing war, there never was a war of religion but since Christianity: for which we are beholden to the Pope."[18] Since the Pope will not grant liberty of conscience to the commonwealth, it in its turn cannot grant this freedom to its subjects; for no government can give what it does not have. The liberty of the people in matters of conscience resides in the liberty of the magistrate in the same regard. People must learn this important truth, and Harrington believes that they should be able, in his quaint phrase, "to distinguish between the shriek of the lapwing and the voice of the turtle."

Harrington dealt with two last and related problems of commonwealths in "Preliminaries I," but these subjects—the courts and civil laws—seemed to him to present less difficulty and are accorded less importance in his theoretical treatment of commonwealths. In this section he warned against lawyers whose interests are wrapped up in the present and the past; because of this concern, they invariably try to perpetuate only what they know; therefore, the construction of a "new-modeled" commonwealth will fail if they are involved in its development.

Lawyers would be of little use in a well-ordered commonwealth. Good commonwealths have few laws and the citizens know them well enough to dispense with the services of lawyers in most instances. Moreover, lawyers are not well disposed to this form of government; for, of all kinds of government, commonwealths always have the fewest laws. On this theoretical or abstract level Harrington says little about the courts. When he does observe that the court systems of various governments offer a great deal of variety, Venice is once more cited as an authoritative example. To Harrington, courts should be so carefully constructed that the arbitrary power granted them is more likely to be used in the efficient pursuit of justice than to do harm.

Harrington's ideal, equal commonwealth has become, in his spinning out of it, a form of authority. The best of the best, it naturally developed out of the balance; and, superficially, it is well within the normative tradition of Aristotle and Richard Hooker. We have already seen, in examining the balance in relation to Aristotle, how the similarities between that concept and Aristotle's treatment of the relationship of property to power are more apparent than real. In developing the superiority of the commonwealth, Harrington deals the same kind of blow to the traditional meaning of "reason." Michael Oakeshott says of Harrington's variety of reason: "It is a faculty of calculation by which men conclude one thing from another and discover fit means of attaining given ends not themselves subject to the criticism of reason, a faculty by which a world believed to be a machine could be made intelligible."[19] With this definition of reason, it is easy to identify reason with interest and then to produce a system of obstacles and checks to the un-bridled pursuit of given and selfish ends. This definition of reason is at the bottom of Harrington's distrust of special groups as custodians of the common interest. Harrington used the vocabulary of the Medieval and Classical tradition, which associates reason and virtue. But virtue, too, is not what it had been. It is not love of what is good; it is, instead, a kind of canniness, the ability to reason, to calculate well and cleverly the advantage of the state. But even in making such calculations, those possessing reason and virtue will mix their own advantage with the common interest. They must be carefully watched.

V *Controversy and the Commonwealth*

Despite a number of attacks on the theory of balance, Harrington never seriously altered the specifics of the theory; he contented himself with more and more forceful assertions of its validity. The case he made for the equal commonwealth encountered more criticism, and these attacks took place on the theoretical level (that is, concerning the arguments and exposition contained in the "Preliminaries I") and also in reference to the specific model of the commonwealth that Harrington drew up for England. Defense of the commonwealth on both levels occupied more of Harrington's time than any other controversy and also inspired his best efforts. What we must determine is whether Harrington made any substan-tial alterations in his commonwealth principles in order to counter these criticisms.

There are, in the remainder of the *Oceana*, some additional con-siderations of commonwealths on the theoretical level that not only strengthen points contained in the "Preliminaries" but also an-ticipate some criticisms. In the "Model of the Commonwealth," Harrington expanded on the importance of the ballot. Arguments supporting secrecy and fairness were repeated, and he remarked that ". . . there is in this way of suffrage no less than a demonstration that it is the most pure: and the purity of the suf-ferage in a popular government is the health, if not the life of it; seeing the soul is no otherwise breathed into the soverain power, than by the sufferage of the people."[20]

Harrington also returned to Machiavelli to make two points in reference to commonwealths. He included a lengthy quotation from the *Discourses* to indicate that commonwealths for preservation are

generally peaceful while those for increase have tumults. Commonwealths for preservation have foreign problems because of their
general weakness; commonwealths for increase have domestic
problems because of the attention they must give to foreign affairs.
The problem of balancing the advantages and disadvantages involved is serious, for Machiavelli felt that this problem had no solution. Harrington argued that an equal commonwealth could accomplish this balance. It would be strong in its relationships with its
rivals, and the widespread and generally equal distribution of landed property would eliminate the tumult at home.

The second statement attributed to Machiavelli received kinder
treatment from Harrington. In the *Discourses*, Machiavelli
speculated on the remedy for the relative inefficiency of commonwealths during periods of danger and crises. "Whence
Machiavel concludes it positively, that a commonwealth un-
provided of such a refuge, must fall to ruin: for her course is either
broken by the blow, in one of those cases, or by herself, while it
startles her out of her orders."[21] Harrington, who agreed, states
that, while a dictatorship is contrary to the whole idea of a commonwealth, it is occasionally necessary. There must, however, be a
provision in the orders of the state to insure that the dictator
operates within established limits no matter how serious the danger.
In no case was the creation of a dictator to be left to chance, and the
tenure of this officer was not to exceed the provisions of the rotation.

The first attack on Harrington's commonwealth, executed by Dr.
Ferne, has already been examined. Harrington's responses were
succinct restatements of what had been contained in the
"Preliminaries"; but, in the case of the charge that Israel was not a
commonwealth of the type that Harrington alleged, new ground
was broken. Ferne had argued that the Sanhedrin was not a senate
for the purpose of debating and proposing to the people. The laws
of the Hebrews had come from God, not from a senate; therefore,
these laws had not been chosen by the people. Harrington's reply is
indicative not only of his attitude toward the clergy but of the
pleasure he took in argument and controversy. He used Ferne's own
weapon, the Bible; but his interpretation of selected quotations indicated that the people had a free will and could have refused the
law of God; that, even after they had received God's law, the
Sanhedrin had to propose others, since the laws of God did not
cover every situation. In reply to Dr. Ferne's contention that there

could have been no contract between God and the Hebrews because they were not equals, Harrington said that parties to a contract need not be equal, that even a king could contract for wax.

Harrington was so successful in countering Dr. Ferne's brief and clumsy criticisms that another critic, anonymous this time, writing in *Mercurius Politicus*, remarked that Harrington must have offered to settle Dr. Ferne in "a fat bishoprick" if the doctor would promise to write against *Oceana*. However, a second critic was more effective. Matthew Wren, son of the bishop of Ely, published *Considerations on Mr. Harrington's Commonwealth of Oceana* in 1657. Harrington's ideas had provoked members of a circle of university scholars and intellectuals, and Wren was one of these. In addition to a challenge to the validity of the balance, Wren's book also attacked the equal commonwealth. Harrington, who had been criticized by the clergy for writing about religion, was now the target of the universities because he had written about philosophy and political theory.

He counterattacked in a book of his own, *The Prerogative of Popular Government,* in November 1657. The first part of this work responds to specific criticisms of Wren; the second is a long and rather dreary discussion of ordination, the administration of holy orders, that was written to confound two clerics who, while not concerned with Harrington, had written books about this subject. Harrington had harsh words for the university savants, whom he accused of slander and of an inconsistency that reduced them to the level of "pickpockets." The clerics, Drs. Hammond and Seaman, who were in favor of maintaining a close relationship between church and king, were treated somewhat more gently.

The Prerogative, which is angry and polemical throughout, contains answers to the questions raised in the "Preliminaries" that relate to the equal commonwealth. Wren had gone to the heart of Harrington's argument and questioned the existence of such a thing as a "government of laws." He also attacked the concept of "common interest" and challenged the contention that an equal commonwealth was superior to a monarchy. These criticisms are interesting because they were influenced by Hobbes and owe little to traditional political philosophy. In them, one contemporary or "modern" theorist is criticizing another.

The law, for Wren, is merely the will of the man or men who possess the sovereign power: "To say that laws do or can govern, is to amuse ourselves with a form of speech, as when we say time, or age, or death dos such a thing; to which indeed the phansy of poets, and superstition of women, may adapt a person, and give a power of action; but wise men know they are only expressions of such actions or qualifications as belong to things or persons."[22] Wren thought Harrington was guilty of naiveté in believing that simply because a law originated with the many rather than with one or a few, it was in any way really different. In Wren's view, law is reduced, in all cases, to the level of power; Harrington agreed that this was so in all cases save one. In an equal commonwealth, power was raised to the level of law.

Neither man accepts the traditional definition of law—that it is an ordinance of right reason that is enacted, either implicitly or explicitly, by the sovereign. The only association made by either man of law to reason was made by Harrington in another context. We have seen that the "reason" Harrington had in mind was merely the interest, aided by wit and cleverness, of those who held the balance.

The "interest of mankind" was another concept challenged by Wren. Harrington's use of Hooker to justify his claim that such an interest exists is given short shrift by Wren: "Mr. Hooker's expression is altogether figurative; and it is easier to prove from thence that things wanting sense make discourses, and act by election, than that there is such a thing as a common interest of mankind."[23] Harrington replied that all civil law acknowledges the existence of a common interest and that all civil laws proceed from the nature of man. Men are punished when they do injury to others in the pursuit of selfish interests, and this punishment is universally performed in the public or common interest. Wren reserved some of his most biting satire for the method of proposing and resolving used in the Harringtonian commonwealth to uncover the common interest: ". . . the author of Oceana, that has seen foren countries, convers'd with the speculativi, learn'd of the most serene lady Venetia to work with bobbins, makes you a magistracy like a pippin py, and fells butterprints with S.P.Q.R.? . . . must your mother, who was never there herself, seek you in the oven? com, when I live to see Machiavel in pufpaste, a commonwealth com out of a bakehouse, where smocks were the boulters, let me be a mill-horse. . . ." Wren also turned another one of Harrington's homely examples against its author; if six of twenty men would have the talent to justify the creation of a senate to house them, perhaps one exceptional man should have a monarch's crown? If one becomes king, replied Harrington, it would be with the consent of the others; but what if they refuse? "Why in coms a gallant with a file of musketeers; what, says he, are you dividing and chusing here? go to, I will have no dividing, give me all. Down go the pots, and up go their heels: what is this? why a king! what more? by divine right! as he took the cake from the girls."

The eighth and ninth chapters of the *Prerogative* deal with Wren's charges that no commonwealth would be without sedition, contrary to Harrington's claim that an equal commonwealth would be, and Wren's assertion that a perfect monarchy could avoid that flaw. Regarding the first, Wren simply says that, "Where there is one ambitious poor man, or one viscious rich man, it is impossible there should be any such government as can be secure from sedition."[24] To Harrington, sedition requires more than one ambitious or vicious man; it requires a party of men. Men must, continued Harrington, not only want to overthrow the government or the balance but also have the wherewithal to do so. Nor are Wren's fears about the less rich pulling down the rich given much weight by Harrington. The people themselves are not levelers, he said; and though, in a good commonwealth, they have a vote and the right to participate, they would not use this power to level the rich. The method of proposing and resolving would make such action impossible legally; and the gain, less than ten pounds per annum in rent per person divided equally among the people, wouldn't be worth a revolution.

The claim that the perfect commonwealth would be free from sedition struck Wren as a claim to immortality. He described this form of the commonwealth as being akin to a perpetual motion machine: "Nature has a tendency to make her creature immortal, if it were in the capacity of the matter on which she has to work," says Galen in Harrington's quote, "but the people never dys. This motion of theirs is from the hand of a perpetual mover."[25] Therefore if prudence be applied, as Machiavelli has advised, there is no reason why the banks it erects to contain the flood should not stand as long as the river flows.

Wren criticized two additional aspects of the equal commonwealth: the agrarian, and rotation in office. To a considerable degree, these criticisms had been anticipated by Harrington in *Oceana*, and his response to Wren broke little new ground. The practical criticisms do not get to the level of the real difference between the two theorists. For Wren, agrarian was an unnatural or artificial regulation; and, like every unnatural regulation, it would overturn natural processes, thwart them in their course, and produce illsuited and dangerous conditions. To Harrington, who foresaw a state that could be more controlled and determined by men, all arrangements in societies were, in a sense, artificial and contrived; and the recognition of this essential fact was the secret to establishing a commonwealth. All so-called natural development after a commonwealth had been established would lead, therefore, to something worse. In other words, the developments that would lead to the building of the basis of a commonwealth had to be halted when that development had been completed. The existence of a commonwealth is often proof that other superstructures have failed to find a method of preserving the foundations on which they were built and maintained. The possibility for accomplishing this control exists in a commonwealth because it can be founded on law, a law that is in the interest of all instead of only one or a few.

Though these criticisms of the agrarian stem from both philosophical and practical differences of opinion between Wren and Harrington, those concerning the rotation in office are all based upon the most practical considerations. In some instances, fresh and different arguments are elicited from Harrington. For instance, when Wren says that rotation is only a copy of the system used in Venice, Harrington adds to his theory of commonwealths: "A Political is like a natural body. Commonwealths resemble and differ, as men resemble and differ; among whom you shall not see two faces, or two dispositions, that are alike."[26] When Wren argued that the rotation was not prudent because it would mandate the giving up of office by the best men and when he cited the practice of ancient commonwealths that often turned good men away, Harrington replied that such greatness could overawe a commonwealth and do it great harm. A good commonwealth does not need men of this stripe.

Wren exhibited an antidemocratic bias in a criticism of the rotation when he charged that the only qualification for office under such a system is merely the "art in canvassing for the suffrage of the people." Unlike earlier systems in commonwealths, Harrington's would prohibit such canvassing in an equal commonwealth because he, too, considered this activity to be beneath the dignity of gentlemen and to be dangerous for the state.

There are many examples, wrote Wren, of commonwealths that felt the need to overturn the rotation: ". . . for the hazard of trusting affairs in weak hands then appearing, no sample has been made to trample upon this order." Harrington, who quoted from Machiavelli's *Discourses* to point out the danger in such a suspension of rotation, noted that short-run interests could be served by keeping an excellent official in office but that, in the long run, the commonwealth would suffer from the growth in power of officials retained in this way. They would build up followings and dependents whose loyalty to the official would rival and then overcome their loyalty to the commonwealth. The dilemma is clear: the commonwealth would injure itself either by gaining the habit of violating its own rules (that is, the rotation) or by forcing the retirement of effective generals and other officials.

Wren has one more practical criticism of the rotation: ". . . by taking off at the end of one year som officers, and all at the end of three, will keep the republic in perpetual minority, no man having time allowed him to gain that experience, which may serve to lead the commonwealth to the understanding of her true interest at home or abroad." Actually the rotation would not take "off" all the officers at the end of three years but only one-third, as is the case each year. Harrington believed that the true interest could be discerned in the space of three years or less, especially if the legislative body met in continuous session instead of intermittently as was the case with Parliament. Harrington came to the conclusion that these continuous sessions were vital if the assembly and the senate were to hold their own against the magistracy.

The second part of the *Prerogative*, mentioned before as the arena for a battle between Harrington and two clerics over ordination, compensates its readers for a lack of style with an excess of seriousness. No doubt it was important for Harrington to establish the democratic origins of the biblical priesthood in the face of clerical attempts to place ordination beyond the reach of the vulgar masses or, given the circumstances in England during the 1650s, the Puritans. The point at issue was the translation of two Greek words, *chirontonia* and *chirothesia*, and their use in biblical accounts of the naming of priests and of magistrates. Harrington translates *chirotonia* as "popular suffrage" and *chirothesia* as "laying on of hands." Harrington's contention was that God in the Old Testament instituted *chirotonia* (popular suffrage) both for the commonwealth and for the monarchy of Israel as the method of electing the Sanhedrin as well as the king. As for the New Testament, Harrington believed that he had found an extension of this method in the selection of priests and bishops in the early church. The clerics thought that election and ordination were two different things, but Harrington believed they were parts of the same process.

Although the issue was not settled in the second part of the *Prerogative*, Harrington established himself as a careful student of the Bible, and as an anticlerical theorist; he demonstrated, to the satisfaction of some, perhaps, that the Bible need not be taken exclusively as evidence of God's preference for the monarchical form of government. A continuing thread in Harrington's work is the use of the Bible to show that there is either divine support for the form of the commonwealth and its processes or that, at the very least, nothing in the form of the commonwealth contradicts the divine will as revealed in the Bible. Despite his occasionally awesome displays of scholarship, such demonstrations left his clerical readers unconvinced. Harrington's attitude toward the Bible was altogether too secular for them; he was, after all, infringing on their territory for the express purpose, among other things, of diminishing their power and prestige.

After the publication of the *Prerogative*, Harrington embarked upon a campaign to popularize his ideas and to counter his critics by writing a series of pamphlets. In 1658 Harrington published *The Stumbling-Block of Disobedience, The Seven Models of a Commonwealth*, and a second edition of *Oceana*.[27] The first of these shorter works, *The Stumbling-Block*, contained a restatement of his arguments in support of commonwealths; but he emphasized historical and biblical sources rather than the philosophical justifications that had played such a great role in his refutation of Matthew Wren. Harrington was writing in response to a work that was critical of John Calvin's belief that popular magistrates could rightfully oppose the licentiousness of kings. In this context, Harrington sought to establish the proper claim of such popular magistrates to rule. Though the work is only eight pages long in *Works*, Harrington quotes from the Bible (Judges, Numbers, Exodus, Deuteronomy, Samuel, Hosea, Jeremiah, and Matthew), Calvin, Livy, Aristotle, and Grotius to make his point.

Shortly after the death of Oliver Cromwell on September 3, 1658, Harrington's *Seven Models of a Commonwealth* appeared. The purpose of this work was contained in the longer form of its title, "or brief Directions shewing how a fit and perfect Model of popular Government may be made, found or understood." Harrington condensed what he had written before on this subject and provided summary descriptions of the commonwealths of Israel, Sparta, Athens, Rome, Venice, Holland, and an imaginary English commonwealth. "There is nothing more apparent," he wrote, "than that this nation is greatly disquieted and perplex'd thro a complication of two causes: the one, that the present state therof is not capable of any other form than that only of a popular government; the other, that they are too few who understand what is the form or model naturally necessary to a popular government, or what is requir'd in that form or prudence for the fitting of it to the use of this nation."[28]

In the year following, 1659, Harrington began the most active phase of his career as a political man, polemicist, and organizer. Two more short pamphlets were published in May of that year. Neither *Pour enclouer le canon* nor *A Discourse upon this saying* . . . is primarily philosophical or theoretical, but each is brief and to the point—England is best fitted to be a commonwealth, and it should be an equal commonwealth for reasons already cited by Harrington.[29] He does, however, warn of some dangers that may be embedded in the form of a commonwealth. In *Pour enclouer* he expressed concern about the development of an oligarchy, which would be composed of a second or upper legislative body not elected by the people. Even if such a body were elected by the people, it might be a menace if its members were elected for life or if the form of the commonwealth were not equal and if the people were divided up into tribes that were no more than economic classes.

The complete statement upon which *A Discourse* was written is "The Spirit of the Nation is not yet to be trusted with Liberty; lest it introduce Monarchy, or invade the Liberty of Conscience." Harrington is at his best in this work; there are no wasted words; and the force of the argument, that indeed only the people can be trusted with liberty, is well developed. After quoting "Put not your trust in Princes," he observed that nowhere are Christians told by God not to trust the people. Instead, God tells His people to select only wise and good men to rule in politics and in religion. God does not command, in political matters, either action or a constitution that are contrary to human prudence. The people can be trusted.

The alternatives to trusting the people are stark. Neither kings nor oligarchies have been shown in history to be worthy of a people's trust. They have usually ruined either the people or the nation. "A people under a yoke which they have lost all hopes of breaking, are of a broken, a slavish, a pusillanimous spirit, as the paisant in France. A people under a yoke which they are not out of hopes to break, are of an impatient, of an active, and of a turbulent spirit, as . . . the English, of the ruin of the nobility, under the late monarchy."[30] The danger that is so often feared in the rule of the people vanishes if the people are entrusted with their own liberty under law.

Both of these works were a response to the resignation in 1659 of Richard Cromwell from his position of lord protector. He had gained this precedence after the death of his father with the support of the army, but his rule had been marked by a weakness and an indecision that had not characterized his father. When the Rump of the Long Parliament was called into session, its first move was to gain Richard's resignation. After this feat was accomplished, the Rump Parliament began to consider various proposals for the settlement of England's political crisis. Harrington and others of his mind excitedly began to agitate for the establishment of a commonwealth. This intent explains the brevity, and summary style, of the pamphlets. Like other philosophers and theorists, Harrington believed that, once the world had been explained and understood, the next task was to change it. The man of thought completes himself by becoming a man of action.

While this exciting diversion was occurring in the public world, Harrington was also writing a longer piece in his study, which emerged from the printer in June 1659. Entitled *The Art of Lawgiving*, it contained three books that again considered the general foundation of all governments, the biblical commonwealth of Israel, and a proposed commonwealth for England.[31] Prior to *The Art of Lawgiving* Harrington had contended with clerics and Monarchists, although he had also criticized Cromwell indirectly. Harrington now widened his field of fire to include not only his old adversary Wren, who had published a second book, *Monarchy Asserted*, but also *The Agreement of the People*, a document attributed to the political left in England during the civil war. *The Agreement* was originally written in 1647, when the parliamentary army had been without pay and would no longer accept orders. Several regiments that were heavily influenced by the Levellers chose representatives that submitted *The Agreement* to Cromwell as a basis for a political settlement. The document contained the Leveller program for reform, which, in turn, derived much from the thought of John Lilburne. The program consisted, first of all, of a social contract that originated with all the people and denied the authority of the Parliament, which would not, or could not, pay its army. It was also a radical, democratic constitution for England. Rejected by Cromwell, *The Agreement* went through several revisions, and its potent assertions on behalf of democracy became a challenge to Harrington's basic assumptions and to his proposed commonwealth. *The Art of Lawgiving* was to steer a middle course between the extremes of the Monarchists and the Levellers.

Harrington, in the preface of this work, responds to what was one of the most popular arguments of his age in favor of monarchy: that it corresponds to what was taken to be the natural, patriarchal, structure of the family. We find this case made, among others, by Robert Filmer in his *Patriarcha*. In a society dominated by that type of family, the apparent congruity of family and state satisfied the expectations of prejudice and experience. Harrington, surprisingly, observes that families need not be patriarchal; they could just as easily be equal. If every member of a family had an income sufficient to his needs, no single member could pretend to be lord and master of the others. This family commonwealth could not easily be changed back into the previous monarchical or patriarchal family. This rather advanced idea was a prefigurement, perhaps, of the bourgeois family of our own age. The extension of the balance, under these circumstances, to the family is evidence not only of Harrington's confidence in its validity but also of the precedence that economic and power realities must take over other motivations, such as love and the experience of community.

When Harrington considered the proposals of the Levellers in the third book of *The Art of Lawgiving*, he discussed in the section "The Anarchy of the Levellers" the establishment of a simple representative body of four hundred persons elected by the people. Such a system of representation, Harrington believed, would lead to oligarchy because four hundred men could not accurately represent five hundred thousand. The number was inadequate, and there was no insurance that those selected would be properly qualified. The unrepresentative and possibly incompetent character of this assembly would be partly remedied by the shortness of the term served by these representatives; they would sit for not more than eight months out of the two year term. The remedy was not complete because there was no provision for preventing the death of the body at the end of the term; instead, a council was to be elected by the body to provide whatever continuity would be needed. This arrangement would, in Harrington's opinion, create anarchy. "Government should be establish'd upon a rock, not set upon a precipice."[32] The Levellers proposed a system that would limit sovereignty, but their limited sovereignty would produce a weak and unstable government. The secret of strong and honest government was not the holding back or breaking up of sovereignty but the construction of orders in which no one could find cause or means for the invasion or disturbance of the government.

The Levellers, given Harrington's view, created additional problems for the state they proposed by restricting the use of militia outside of the country. This restriction invited the creation of, and ultimately, dependence upon, mercenary troops. Whenever a man hired someone to replace him in the military forces he was, in reality, hiring his own master. No commonwealth could prosper were it to require hired soldiers for its defense.

Harrington finally took up cudgels against his old adversary, Matthew Wren, in the conclusion to *The Art of Lawgiving*. The tone was set when Harrington began this section with the assertion that even commonwealths that are incorrectly ordered are less seditious than even the best of monarchies. This statement moved the case for the commonwealth beyond the point attained before. Having epitomized the commonwealth, he then took up Wren's new criticisms, which were that Harrington's equal commonwealth was logical and contained no contradictions but was a lie because it did not conform to nature. To Wren, the basic inequality that exists among men would not be remedied in an equal commonwealth, the sources of sedition would remain, and the representatives of the people in the assembly and in the senate would be tempted to seize all power. Moreover, Harrington's prejudice against lawyers, clerics, and doctors which had been manifested in his unwillingness to allow them to participate in politics and military affairs, was unfair and ill-advised.

In Harrington's reply to Wren, he said that an equal commonwealth was proven by history to be in conformity with nature, and his equal commonwealth had not been proposed to eliminate evil or ignorance among men but to prevent these from influencing government. The people's representatives would not try to assume the power because they already possessed it and did so with the consent of the people. If the people overthrew this system, the power would revert to all the people instead of remaining with the assembly and senate. As for men in the professions, they were too narrow in training and interest to be trusted in the making of laws or the conducting of war; there was honor enough for them in the practice of their professions.

The most serious discussion of Wren's ideas by Harrington concerned his assertion of monarchy. The basis of Wren's argument was that, since sedition was always a clear and present danger in any state, the sovereign required the united force of the subjects to suppress it. When this force was vested in a natural person, as in a monarchy, rather than in an artificial government created by many men, which was the case in a commonwealth, the task of suppressing sedition was simplified and more efficiently performed. Of this Harrington said, "Who reads Mr. Hobbs, if this be news? But what provision is made by either of these authors, that the forces of these subjects must needs be united?"[33] Wren and Hobbes wished to supply that want by creating a nobility, but a nobility that would be inferior in power and glory to the monarchy. Wren would accomplish this inferiority by placing a series of restrictions on the nobility and by providing his king with an army and castles with moats throughout the country. This proposal was an old one for Harrington, and he disposed of it with dispatch: "What then remains but to say, that Mr. Wren having declar'd the perfection of monarchical government to consist in a mixture of monarchy by a nobility, and a monarchy by arms, has as to his model intirely subverted monarchy?" To Harrington, either the nobility or the army would ultimately destroy this monarchy.

Even after the publication of *The Art of Lawgiving*, the controversies involving Harrington continued. These differences of opinion were most frequently based on his specific proposals for an English commonwealth on the model of *Oceana* and were not often concerned with the abstract principles of the balance and the form of the equal commonwealth. His adverse critics continued to be a diverse lot, for various Royalists, clerics from different segments of the established church, university scholars, and, in the last months before the restoration of the house of Stuart, his own allies among the commonwealthmen and an occasional Fifth Monarchy man attacked his ideas.

In regard to the form of the equal commonwealth, these controversies brought forth many restatements from Harrington of his earlier arguments. These were successively more refined, but little of substance was altered. As the excitement of the times increased, Harrington was prone to inflate his promises on behalf of the com-

monwealth: "If your commonwealth be rightly instituted, seven
years will not pass, ere your clusters of parties, civil and religious,
vanish; not through any force, as when cold weather kills flies; but
by the rising of greater light, as when the sun puts out
candles. . . . England shall raise her head to ancient glory, the
heavens shall be of the old metal, the earth no longer lead, nor shall
the sounding air eternally renounce the trumpet of fame."[34] As
criticisms mounted, Harrington was less and less apt to be modest
about his contribution to political discourse: "If these models (in
which I claim to be the first that had laid the whole, and the highest
mystery's of the antient commonwealths, the lowest capacity of
vulgar debate) be not all in the months of great men, and in
pamphlets, for chimeras or utopias, it is great change."[35] Despite
the increasing effectiveness of his literary style in the pamphlets and
other shorter works, the two great characteristics of Harrington's
political thought—the balance and the equal commonwealth—remain as they stood when first seated in the "Preliminaries" of
Oceana.

VI   *Harrington and the Origin of the Equal Commonwealth*

The difficulty we have in establishing a context for the equal
commonwealth is similar to the problem that Harrington faced in
convincing his readers that such an entity had ever existed. His
critics accused him of constructing either an imaginary commonwealth or of simply imitating the institutional structure of
Venice. When Harrington, as we have seen, denied both charges,
his description of the equal commonwealth depended upon a mixture of experience gleaned in his European travels and from his own
very wide reading of contemporary and ancient historians and
political theorists.

Unfortunately, the Venice Harrington could have known from his
own experience was no longer a commonwealth. Most of what
Harrington said about the Venetian Commonwealth was based
upon Gasparo Contarini's *The Commonwealth and Government of
Venice*, Niccolo Machiavelli's *Prince* and *Discourses*, Francesco
Guicciardini's *Storia d'Italia*, and Donato Giannotti's *Libro de la
republica de Vinitiani*. Of these, Contarini's book seems to have had
the greatest influence upon Harrington's evaluation of Venice
because his misconceptions are similar to the distortions found in
Contarini. Harrington was convinced that Venice, at the time he

wrote *Oceana,* was an equal commonwealth and that it had been so for centuries. This evidence he produced on several occasions to support his contention that, properly ordered, an equal commonwealth might be immortal. Since he was almost completely mistaken after having spent considerable time in the city, he must have been misled by the charm and persuasiveness of Contarini's narrative, by the distractions of the city itself, or by his own need for an ideal in touch with reality. The last two possibilities are more understandable than the first; for Contarini's influence, not only on Harrington but on many other English commonwealth supporters, requires explanation.

Gasparo Contarini, a cardinal of the Roman Catholic church, was a member of an eminent Venetian family which claimed eight doges among its number. Contarini's *The Commonwealth and Government of Venice,* printed and circulated in 1543, immediately gained wide popularity but was probably no more avidly read anywhere than in Venice itself. Contarini, a loyal citizen, described his city and its constitution in such glowing terms that his English translator—an English version of the book appeared in 1599—remarked that the Grand Council "seemeth to bee an assembly of Angels." Other accounts indicate that it was not.[36]

Although other histories heaped praise on Venice, Contarini's was exceptional because he described the constitution as changeless; his Venice was a city governed by an aristocracy of virtue established by a great lawgiver. As a result of Contarini's work, Venice was perceived as the immortal manifestation of the mixed constitution with elements of monarchy, of aristocracy and democracy, or of assembly, senate, and magistracy. He consciously established links between Venice and the ancient commonwealths so eloquently celebrated in Polybius, Livy, and Plutarch. Venice, in his hands was the culmination of the art of creative politics; timeless and immutable, its government was a miracle of stability in a world of flux. To create this ideal, Contarini ignored obvious alterations in the institutions of Venice and, in the view of one modern historian, indulged in obvious misrepresentations. This was the Venice that Harrington knew and used as the exemplifier of republican institutions.

Other continental writers who, like Contarini, praised Venice, were translated into English and their books were popular. Besides those mentioned above, Paolo Paruta, Thomas de Fougasses, Bernardo Guistiniani, Pietro Guistiniani, Andrea Mauroceni, Giovanni

Botero, and others were all familiar to English readers. All of them wrote about politics, Italy, and Venice; and their generally favorable references became part of the climate of opinion in England. So much was this the case that critics of Venice in England and even in Europe were rare, and they made little headway in their attempts to correct the distortions of Contarini and the others. In England, the antipapal foreign policy of the Venetians may have enhanced their reputation with Protestants.

The foremost European critic of Venice and Contarini was Jean Bodin, who was admired and often quoted by Harrington. Bodin pointed out that Venetian institutions had changed much in the history of the city, that the city had often been torn by internal strife, that until shortly before Contarini its government had been a pure monarchy, and that Venice was now (c.1600) a pure aristocracy. Harrington apparently missed all this, not only while he was in Venice, but also when he read Bodin.

Only after Venice had become a symbol of the ideal commonwealth during the civil war did English criticism of its government begin. Prior to that, only praise existed, and such writers as the poet George Wither, author of *A poem concerning a perpetuall parliament;* James Howell, who wrote *Survay of the signorie of Venice;* and Harrington perpetuated the myth of Venice. Robert Filmer, in other ways the unconscious confirmer of popular prejudices, challenged and criticized the myth in his *Observations upon Aristotle's Politics.* Marchamont Needham, writing after *Oceana* was published and after Harrington was retired, was blunt: "In Venice the people are excluded from all share in government, from making laws and from bearing offices. 'Tis rather a Junta than a Commonwealth."[37] Harrington traveled in Europe without having heard and without hearing criticism of Venice. In this atmosphere, it is not so difficult to understand why he noted no flaw in the government of the city while he was resident there. His attitude toward Venice was a product of the generally held opinion of his time; against this only the most dramatic evidence to the contrary would have been sufficient to create doubt. We may deduce from this that during his stay there Venice exhibited only its serene side to Harrington.

Of the institutions of the equal commonwealth, the assembly, the senate, and the magistracy were all sufficiently discussed by so many authors in so many contexts that Harrington could have found them anywhere and also have received reinforcement for their advisability in any number of other books. Although the many books about Venice claimed to see this constellation of institutions there, the mixed constitution can be found in Plato's *Laws*, Aristotle's *Politics*, and Polybius' *Histories*. But of these theorists Polybius claimed most for it; for by relating this constitution to the division of government functions, what has come to be called "checks and balances," he felt justified in claiming permanence and stability for it. Cicero celebrated this constitution in his orations, and Plutarch's *Lives* contained encomiums in honor of the men who built and maintained the ancient commonwealths. For Harrington, who always looked for unity and consistency, the prospects presented by this degree of agreement was most appealing.

Elections and ballots as well as the rotation were processes found in various commonwealths. Harrington had only to collect descriptions of the processes and balance the practicality of the methods against the liberty he wished to maintain, the uniting of power and interest he wished to achieve, and the fear he had of entrenched personal power. We can take at face value his claim to have discovered the system of proposing and choosing, or rather of debating and resolving, by observing a similar method employed by children to settle such disputes.

The agrarian and the combination of a national church with freedom of conscience, two more aspects of Harrington's equal commonwealth, are not so easy to trace. Some writers have noted that Harrington was not the first in England to recognize the need and benefit for ensuring a broad distribution of land ownership. In *The Agreement of the People*, the Levellers had advocated establishing a limit on the amount of land an individual could own. Aristotle had argued the advisability, in both a private and a public moral sense, of regulating the amount and use of property. Harrington said he had been most impressed by what had happened to commonwealths that had omitted the agrarian from its orders. The balance recognized the relation between power and wealth; the achievement of stability and permanence made the agrarian a necessity.

Despite the present arrangement of church-state relationships in Great Britain, Harrington's proposal for the settlement of this issue on the principles of both an established church and religious toleration still seems somewhat contrived. Nor does his explanation, related above, seem at all satisfactory. Of course, almost every state had an established church; and even England had retained one despite the vicissitudes and the difficulty of putting the name of Presbyterian or Episcopalian on it. Harrington says many fine things about the importance of religion, and even about the need for churches as sources of order and education. This praise coupled with his extensive use of the Bible, has led one scholar to say that Harrington was a Puritan and an Independent on religious matters and that his proposals reflect this state of mind.[38] Others declare him to have been essentially secular in outlook: he was practical enough to see that religion was quite useful, in a Machiavellian way, for the state, and he was experienced enough to see that more could be gained by granting room in the community for peaceful dissenters.

More intriguing is the attempt of biographers to attribute Harrington's religious tolerance to one of his teachers at Oxford, William Chillingworth, Doctor of Divinity, who had been a Roman Catholic but who had joined the Church of England while still young. His book, *The Religion of the Protestants a Safe Way to Salvation*, was a response to those Catholics who attacked him for his apostasy; its tone was indicative of his effectiveness as a controversialist; but he was, however, noted as an advocate of toleration. John Aubrey, who immortalized Chillingworth in his *Brief Lives*, says that Dr. Chillingworth gave Charles I very bad military advice, contracted *morbus castrensis*, and died a much disliked man. "In his sicknesse he was inhumanely treated by Dr. Cheynell, who, when he was to be buryed, threw his booke into the grave with him, saying, 'Rott with the rotten; let the dead bury the dead.' "[39] There is little firm evidence that Harrington received his preference for religious toleration from Chillingworth.

Harrington's equal commonwealth is a child of his study and his creative imagination. He was generous in giving credit to the men who had written about commonwealths, though he claims credit for the ideas he believed to be his. Of the two basic Harringtonian ideas, the balance is rooted in experience and observation, but the principles of the equal commonwealth seem more appropriate to the library.

CHAPTER 4

History, Economics, and Political Science

THE world in which James Harrington lived was violent
and disorderly; both words, so often used interchangeably, are
necessary to understand conditions in the seventeenth century. The
wars of religion, which pitted nation against nation and divided
peoples against themselves, and the civil war in England give
testimony to the violent spirit of the age. Social historians note the
incidence with which individual disputes were submitted, not to
settlement by law but by duel. "The absence of any sure method of
redressing private wrongs, the law being so cumbersome and corrupt, led to the continuation of the personal feud in the unlighted
and unpatrolled streets."[1] Swords were part of a gentleman's daily
attire; and even John Aubrey, James Harrington's gentle and
amiable friend, had reason to express his fear of his enemies in his
diary: "Danger of being killed by William, Earl of Pembroke, then
Lord Herbert, at the election of Sir William Salkeld for New
Sarum." Because of the plague and malnutrition, many of those
who survived the violence died early deaths.

The era was disorderly; a series of challenges and shocks had so
destroyed or so seriously weakened the intellectual and moral consensus that people were not sustained by either quality. Their fear
of violence and death redoubled the feeling, particularly among
well-educated people, that the crisis required a new intellectual
basis for its resolution. For several centuries prior to the Protestant
Reformation, Scholastic philosophy and Roman Catholicism, in-
tegrated since the thirteenth century, had served to justify and to
elaborate an order or priority for Europe. With the growth of
nationalism and the explosion of knowledge both of the ancient past
and of the world and universe, this center could not hold. Nor could
it, given the vigor and discipline of the Counterreformation, be

93

destroyed. In the space of a hundred years, the religious, philosophical, and political order of Europe was replaced with a new and heightened competition in each of these aspects of culture. In another two hundred years, when the Industrial Revolution had rapidly transformed the institutional structure of society, the crisis deepened.

The theme that unites political theorists in every age is the search for unity and deliverance. Everyone who is moved to think with discipline about the chaos that abounds in the realm of politics wants to find the key concept that creates order. Since the chaos of politics is what produces the misery and the suffering of humanity, the abolition of chaos will be mankind's deliverance. In regard to the theory of the balance and the superiority of the equal commonwealth, we have seen the concepts that Harrington has proposed for these purposes; and we have noted that he has claimed a certainty for each that goes beyond that claimed by earlier theorists. As for the evidence upon which Harrington based these claims, he was aware of the intellectual inadequacy of religion and philosophy. He used both in his arguments with his opponents, but neither can be said to be an integral part of his theories. The shortcoming of religion and philosophy was their failure to do more than to establish the principles of individual and public morality for our consideration. There was nothing in either to ensure that these principles would be acted upon by rulers and citizens with any consistency. For earlier political theorists the law, supported by the sovereign power of the state, was to serve this function. Harrington remarked that the association of religion, philosophy, law, and power had been imperfect since the fall of Rome. He proposed that law and power be founded, instead, on an economic relationship, the correctness of which was for him, sustained by history and observation.

This proposal leads many scholars to classify James Harrington as an early social scientist; his obvious affection for history as proof, the economic character of the balance, the elaborate political engineering contained in *Oceana* all combine to lend him that air. Accordingly, some have praised him for this and for the accuracy of his analysis and observations; some have said that neither his analysis nor his observations can be supported by the facts; and still others say that he was not at all a social scientist. In considering James Harrington's theories, we shall examine his view of history, the use he makes of economic observations, and the new science of politics that he believed he had discovered.

I   *The Historian and His Dialectic*

James Harrington wrote about the importance of history and observation to the political thinker and actor: "No man can be a Politician except he be first an Historian or a Traveler; for except he can see what Must be, or May be, he is no Politician: Now if he have no knowledge in story, he cannot tell what hath been; and if he hath not been a Traveller, he cannot tell what is: but he that neither knoweth what hath been, nor what is; can never tell what must be, or what may be."[2] History, which traditional philosophy relegated to a rather insignificant place in the scheme of things, was raised by Harrington to the level of principle. It was the link in his attempt to unify past, present, and future; it provided the knowledge that will ultimately unite thinking and acting in politics.

As much as most men of his time and place, Harrington had traveled; and, with his experience and his contacts at courts in England and in Holland, he had observed politics in the inner circle; therefore, his learning was widely acknowledged by others. Thomas Herbert, who had served as gentleman of the king's bedchamber, said that fellow attendant Harrington was the "best read man in history of all sorts" of his time.[3] The attention he paid to these pursuits shows through all that he wrote, for even when he said that this or that aspect of his plan for England or of his description of the equal commonwealth was based upon "right reason or a natural law, every article of the Constitution of Oceana must be judged at the bar of history before its admission." The primacy claimed for history in this context is unadulterated Machiavelli; but here, as in other matters, Machiavelli is only the starting point for Harrington. In the end, Harrington found that Machiavelli's attitude toward history was inadequate to support the burden of an immortal commonwealth.

Machiavelli saw infinite possibilities for human corruption when he examined the record of humanity, and he found little reason for raising any hope of deliverance from the unfortunate effects of such evil. He did believe, though, that what could be learned from history could serve as a guide to policy in a state more orderly and permanent than those that he had watched rise and fall so frequently in Italy. A set of political rules was his object, tactics and strategies suited to the problems that beset every state periodically. Machiavelli did not hope to end the cyclical development of governments but he did believe that the cycle could be lengthened to the advantage of all. Although he did not hope to eliminate

either human corruption or its impact on politics, he believed that
the prudence that could come from reflecting on carefully chosen
historical examples could be a check upon the dissolution of order.
Throughout his writings, Machiavelli is haunted by the feeling that
human control over human beings is always limited and so is human
control over history. Over half of what happens is laid to 'Fortuna,'
fickle and unpredictable.

Harrington expected to gain more from the study of history than
a set of guidelines or what, in effect, are bromides for a recurring
painful condition in the body politic. Not mere prudence but the
eternal principles of government were what history would yield.
The apparent variety found in the governments of the past would
be resolved if the key could be found—the balance.

Harrington, after Giannotti, divided history into two periods. The
first, which he styled ancient prudence, encompassed all Western
history—especially the separate histories of Israel, Greece, and
Rome—until the end of the Roman Republic and the establishment
of the empire. The second period, which he saw coming to a close so
far as England was concerned, began with the "arms of Caesar"
and extended through the breakup and fall of the Roman Empire
and the Middle Ages to his own time, and this era was called
"modern prudence." The major difference between these two ages
was found in the forms of government that dominated each. In ancient prudence, government was "an Art whereby a Civil Society of
men is instituted and preserved upon the foundation of common
right or interest."[4] Modern prudence, which for Harrington constituted a decline from the superior ancient era, conceived government as "an Art whereby some man, or some few men, subject a
City or a Nation, and rule it according unto his or Their private interest."

The historical event that marked the transition of ancient to
modern prudence was the rise to power of Caesar. For in a sense the
growth of the empire and then the concentration of power in the
hands of a single ruler and his army meant that the Roman
Republic could not be restored and that the earlier republics of
Israel, Sparta, and Athens could not be resurrected. All of these
commonwealths had failed because they were unequal; either the
rotation, the agrarian, the ballot, or the division of functions
between assembly and senate had been improperly ordered. These
faults had inevitably led to a change in the balance—one away from

that which undergirded the commonwealth and toward that of a monarchy.

Harrington equated the monarchy of the Roman Empire with that of Turkey. At first the emperors governed through their soldiery by granting them land in the form of benefices for life. Later these benefices were passed to a man's heirs, if they were willing to serve in the army. This form of balance had, according to Harrington, a fatal flaw: the landholding class that was created caused the emperors to fear for their lives and office. To counter this threat, the Praetorian Guard was created to protect the emperor's power and person. The state that resulted was, in Harrington's felicitous phrase, "neither Hawk nor Buzzard"; and "it made a flight accordingly; and having the avarice of the Souldiery on this hand to satisfie upon the people; and the Senate and the people on the other to be defended from the souldiery; the Prince being perpetually tossed, seldom dyd any other death than by one Horn of this Dilemma."[5]

As time went by, the emperors attempted to remedy this fault by making the benefices hereditary without condition and by distributing the Praetorian Guard throughout the empire. Having thus altered the balance, the emperors then depended upon mercenary forces, usually Goths from Northern Europe. Having descended so far from ordinary prudence, the emperors then went one step farther by defaulting on the payment of tribute or wages to their mercenaries; then the whole of Italy was opened up to the depredations of "Vandals, Huns, Lombards, Franks, and Saxons." These peoples destroyed most of what remained of Rome; "Camillus, Caesar, and Pompey, being come to Edmund, Richard and Geoffrey."

All this unhappiness was the foundation for modern prudence. The Roman Empire was replaced by the Gothic balance, a state composed of three distinct groups of people: a nobility that participated in the royal dignity of the king, possessed cities and castles, and exercised certain powers independent of the king; a lesser nobility whose members owed their place to their superiors and were obligated to serve them and their interests; and an order of private men who owed to the lesser nobility what it, in turn, owed to the nobility. This form of government, said Harrington, was what all the kingdoms of Christendom were when they were first erected.

In our discussion of the balance, we have seen the even more fatal shortcomings of the form of government that was built upon the Gothic balance. With the land, or the power, divided among these three groups so that no single group held the preponderance, the disorders stemming from competition would never cease until a true balance could be created. To achieve it, some group had to gain a preponderance in land ownership and then establish a government that would realize their interest. In the "Preliminaries II" of the *Oceana*, Harrington related how this achievement had come about in England; and, since his analysis of this case is interesting and important, we must examine it momentarily. Suffice it to say for now that Harrington was of the opinion that the preponderance of property now rested with the people, that England was ripe for the establishment of a commonwealth, and that he knew the method by which to ensure that the commonwealth would be equal. Once established, this equal commonwealth would be immortal.

We have, in Harrington's narrative, the creation and operation of a crude dialectic of history. The weaknesses and failures of the first epoch produce a change to the second; the weaknesses and failure of the second result in a third. This development is certainly not a re-creation of the dialectic of Plato, which was a description of how thought develops, not history. It is not yet the sophisticated dialectic of Hegel nor the ideologically potent Marxian dialectic. The Harrington dialectic is not particularly well developed but its form is clear: power and property depend upon each other; inevitably they change until, at last, an equal commonwealth is founded. An equal commonwealth, because it ensures that no change will occur in either the foundation or the superstructure, is the third and last stage of history.

This third era is not a full-fledged millenium. No radical transformation of human nature is anticipated; human beings in an equal commonwealth will not be angels or members of a universal community. Harrington never claims that the equal commonwealth will be the one thousand year reign of Christ upon earth. He is not a secular Joachim of Flora nor a bourgeois Marx, but his view of history moves beyond Machiavelli and implicitly counters the orthodox Christian rejection of the possibility of any immortal government in this world. The traditional antimony between the eternal City of God and the transient City of Man is compromised in the vision of the immortal commonwealth, a possibility contemplated by neither Machiavelli nor Polybius.

II *England and the Gothic Balance*

The event before Harrington's eyes and well fixed in his memory when he began to move toward the concept of *Oceana* was the civil war in England, which culminated with the execution of his friend, Charles I. These tragedies loom large in the writings of several generations of English thinkers and still excite the interest of thinkers and scholars today. Harrington's interpretation of the causes and his prediction of the outcome are the gist of *Oceana* on the most practical level.

In "Preliminaries II," a concise application of the balance as the key to the movement of history appears. The English variety of the Gothic balance was a constellation of earls, barons, thanes, vavasors, sheriffs, and viscounts. Harrington, depending upon accounts written by Sir Edward Coke and Henry Bracton, estimated that between two hundred and two hundred and fifty barons temporal and spiritual were at the pinnacle of the political system. Their lands were divided into approximately sixty thousand knights' fees which could furnish that many men for the king's service. This was almost the whole of the landed property in England. Harrington thought that freeholds in the people—that is, land owned free and clear by people who were not part of the greater or lesser nobility—did not amount to very much. "Wherefore the Ballance and Foundation of this government was in the 60,000 knights fees, and these being possest by the 250 Lords, it was a government of the Few, or of the Nobility; wherein the people might also assembly, but could have no more than a mere name."[6] Harrington was not receptive to the claims made before, during, and after his life that the English monarchy had been any form of commonwealth. In the Gothic balance, the clergy, or Lords Spiritual, who owned a full third of the landed property, weighed far more on the scales of power than the people. The balance described above would simply not support a commonwealth.

This government of the king who ruled together with his lords was as unstable in England as it proved to be elsewhere: "Whence, the kings being as obstinate on the one side for their absolute power, as these [the Lords] on the other for their immunities, grew certaine Wars which tooke their Denomination from the Barons."[7] In order to break the opposition to royal power, the kings tried first of all to gain control of the House of Lords by naming barons by writ which were friendly to the kings' interests. This practice may have seemed a master stroke to some, but it had for Harrington the appearances of disaster, for this tactic, originated by King John, resulted in a "wrestling match" in which the king, when he was stronger, overthrew the balance, and the nobility, when they were stronger, overturned the balance themselves. To complicate matters, Richard II created a third category of barons, those of letters patents, who depended upon the king's own wealth for their maintenance and lent no strength to the throne. The institution of the monarchy suffered less, however, than Richard himself, who was deposed by the landed barons. This deposition became a habit, and the barons henceforth set up and pulled down kings as their interests dictated.

This situation continued until the reign of Henry VII, who, after he had been placed upon the throne as a result of the barons, moved to eliminate, or reduce, their predominance. Harrington thought that Henry's "naturall subtilty" led him to the discovery that "a throne supported by a Nobility, is not so hard to be ascended, as kept warm."[8] Henry took three steps to achieve his ends: by the Statute of Population, he insured the maintenance of every holding of twenty acres or more. The houses were to be kept up, and the land was to be tilled by transferring considerable land into the hands of the "yeomanry and middle people" who no longer depended upon the barons for their property. This redistribution of land had the effect of partially disarming the barons. The second of these acts, the Statute of Retainers, completed the process of disarming by depriving the barons of those dependent knights who served them as cavalry and commanders. Thus reduced, many barons found that country life palled, and they moved to court. This raised their living expenses; and, now finding that the traditional fees from their property were inadequate, they racked their rents and then sold their property for ready money. This last resort for the luxurious and court-loving nobility was created by Henry's Statute of Alienations which permitted ancestral holdings to be disposed of more efficiently than had been the case with entails.

These changes were but the first step in the process that altered the Gothic balance. Henry VIII, by dissolving the abbeys and transferring their lands to new ownership, subtracted yet more from that part of the property that had been used by the barons as a basis of power. By the time of Elizabeth I, it was obvious that the two hundred to two hundred and fifty barons of the Gothic balance no longer held the preponderance and that the people had succeeded to their place. The people could have taken the power that was now, in reality, theirs, but they were "not apt to see their own strength." Elizabeth created a kind of romance between herself and her people—"perpetuall Lovetricks" were exchanged—and the throne was preserved. This illusion served to shore up the eroding monarchy for a while. But James I, called Morpheus by Harrington, perhaps because his policy was slumberous in the face of the rising danger to the throne, did not share Elizabeth's felicitous political style; and his son, Charles I, inherited a realm that had to be governed without the support of the nobility, who were weakened beyond restoration, or of the people, who were now sullen and powerful. "But a monarchy divested of her Nobility, hath no refuge under Heaven, but an Army. Wherefore the dissolution of this Government caused the War, not the war the dissolution of this Government."[9] For the monarchy to survive, it had either to find a balance to support it or to create one.

Having explained the cause of the civil war in terms of gradual economic and institutional change, rather than in one of the ways then common, Harrington then proceeded to show why the restoration of the monarchy was improbable. Confiscations enacted against the English people by an English king would be against any "example in humane Nature," and a confiscation that takes place where many people own land would be dangerous and probably fruitless. History, said Harrington, shows no example of how "the forfeiture of a populous Nation, not conquer'd, but friends, and in cool blood, might be taken."[10] An absolute monarchy is no longer possible without creating the danger of a successful invasion by an enemy. Nor could some combination of people and king be established without its becoming a commonwealth. A monarchy could not be founded upon a balance where the people hold the preponderance. "To conclude, Oceana [England], or any other Nation of no greater extent must have a competent Nobility, or is altogether incapable of Monarchy: for where there is equality of estates, there must be equality of power; and where there is equality of power there can be no monarchy."

III   *The Economist*

In the examination of the principle of the balance, the degree to which Harrington was an economic determinist was an important question. He appeared to be, in his definition of political power, a forerunner of Marx; and his dialectic may be used to confirm the association. His determinism, as we have seen, is not strict. Either the superstructure or the foundation may lead the way in his version of dialectical development. In all of Harrington's theories, the emphasis that is placed on economics is at the bottom of a number of scholarly controversies over the system of economics that he had observed and had anticipated. In other words, was Harrington essentially bourgeois and capitalist or simply a mercantilist? Was he able to see what was emerging as a new economic order in England or was he confirming an economic arrangement that stretched back to the Roman and Athenian republics? How accurate an economic observer was he?

The case for listing Harrington among bourgeois and capitalist thinkers is best made by C. B. MacPherson in *The Political Theory of Possessive Individualism* (1962). It is the key to resolving the contradictions in the applications of the balance that Harrington made in the *Oceana*. MacPherson identifies the balance as a bourgeois idea because relationships between men are viewed in terms of the market, "in which, that is to say, land and labour, as well as moveable wealth and goods made for consumption, are treated as commodities to be bought and sold and contracted for with a view to profit and accumulation, and where men's relations to others are set largely by their ownership of these commodities and the success with which they utilize that ownership to their own profit."[11]

There is more in this vein to be mined; for, contrary to the strictures of medieval society, usury is explicitly praised in Harrington's *The Prerogative of Popular Government* as a necessity in a commonwealth. Without some return on money loaned, it would "rust unprofitably in private purses." When laws favor the borrower over the lender, "as at four in the hundred, or therabouts, usury becomes a mighty profit to the public, and a charity to privat men."[12] Actually Harrington's view of usury was neither medieval nor modern. Usury is not absolutely wrong, and the rightness of it depends upon its utility to the state. In England, where money never overbalances wealth in land, usury is usually safe and may be encouraged; in other lands, in which wealth in land is limited, usury is dangerous. This attitude toward usury is not yet entirely bourgeois.

Harrington looked upon accumulation and profit as the proper reward for industry. The estates that were being built up by what he called "private men"—the gentry and yoemanry—were built upon "industry" rather than upon tenure and fixed rents, inheritance and royal grants. Industry in the sense employed by

Harrington is labor, the mixing of human effort with the land: "Industry of all things is the most accumulative, and accumulation of all things hates levelling: the revenue therfore of the people being the revenue of industry, tho som nobility . . . may be found to have bin levellers, yet not any people in the world."[13] This view of accumulation is certainly a dynamic element introduced, if not for the first time, at least in a rather new way, to economics. Accumulation for accumulation's sake was opposed by traditional moralists as unworthy for human beings, but bourgeois theory in full flower eventually viewed accumulation as the ultimate measure of human success and God's favor.

Once more Harrington falls between two views; perhaps the term "transitional" is the best description of his position. Harrington ignores the question of morality in regard to accumulation through industry, except to say that it is morally superior to accumulation through other means; but any kind of accumulation without institutional limitations is viewed as dangerous for public order in a commonwealth. While medieval thinkers sought to control accumulation through moral suasion, and while bourgeois thinkers sought to release it from such inhibitions, Harrington wanted accumulation freed from an absolute moral restraint and controlled, instead, by prudence and law. Later bourgeois economists proposed through the doctrine of laissez-faire the abolition of legal restraints as well as of moral restraints. Harrington, who had witnessed the gradually weakened grip of morality as a brake upon activity destructive of domestic amity, retained the Aristotelian prejudice against uncontrolled growth in any part of the body politic. He wanted to regulate growth without abolishing it, to provide freedom for individual opportunity without creating a menace to his commonwealth.

As another bourgeois element in Harrington's writings, MacPherson notes the theme of social mobility, of individual improvement, of increasing fluidity in the social economy of England. The working of the dialectic in English history transferred power from the nobility to the "yeomanry and middle men" as the land came, more and more, to be owned by them. But industry and commercial trade were the more specific means employed by these people to rise within society. And, while Harrington used the agrarian to justify the strict limitation of ownership in land, he left estates in money and in goods free to grow. If the countryside was to remain in the hands of a relative few, the cities, particularly London, would become the stage for the second kind of estate that would come into its own. Harrington believed that the enrichment of the cities that would take place—one which had, he thought, already been taking place—would also create occasions for the economic expansion of the countryside: "The more mouths there be in a city, the more meat of necessity must be vented by the country, and so there will be more corn, more cattel, and better markets; which breeding more laborers, more husbandmen, and richer farmers, bring the country so far from a commonwealth of cottagers. . . ." [14] Because an expanding city provides more certain markets, a more dependable and predictable economic environment would develop; and its predictability would be in growth, not in stagnation. The end of history that was foreseen by Harrington in the establishment of the immortal commonwealth would not mean the end of economic improvement.

The question as to whether this economic growth would drive the dialectic to begin its movement again after the establishment of an ideal commonwealth was also considered by Harrington. He realized that such a condition of well-being would also result in an increase in population. Since this "overplus" population would need a livelihood, it could turn either to arms and imperialism or to merchandize and manufacture. In Harrington's immortal commonwealth, for increase they would turn to both; and, "it being necessary that they lay their heads and their stock together, this makes populous citys."

In this view of economics and politics, the land is considered most basic and stable because it would be limited and would impose limits. Merchandize, manufacture, and imperialism would be unlimited and impose no limits. They would follow one another in an ascending spiral toward greatness for the nation. So long as the land remained divided among a number great enough to insure a diversity of interests, the other sources of wealth were no hazard to the commonwealth; they provided a much needed release for the ambitious, talented, but unlanded section of the population.

This commonwealth for increase is what MacPherson terms "The Opportunity State." The opportunities for England to achieve greatness are matched on another level by the opportunities of each individual to achieve his economic independence from a necessity imposed either by nature or by man. This opportunity would not result in leveling; indeed, since wealth and power would depend upon industry—upon "effort intelligently applied to the production of commodities for the market"—citizens would be as resolutely opposed to leveling in the economic realm as they would be committed to it in the political area. This strong commitment to political equality, which Harrington maintained was altogether different from equality in wealth, was necessary to preserve the opportunity state from falling under the domination of an oligarchy. Thus, even though Harrington's agrarian limit, applied to England, could result in as few as five thousand owners with two thousand pounds in land per year and with five hundred thousand unlanded citizens, the equal commonwealth would be maintained through a single interest based upon the economic interdependence of city and countryside and upon the desire of the many to preserve economic opportunity as the basis of expanding individual wealth and national power. MacPherson concludes that the balance would cease to operate in an equal commonwealth because the bourgeois commitment to economic expansion and opportunity would abolish it. The unity Harrington sought would not be achieved through institutions but ultimately through the existence of a new moral and intellectual consensus that would be bourgeois in its attitude toward human relationships and economic theory.

Other critics have been unwilling to accept Harrington as a bourgeois and capitalist theorist. J. G. A. Pocock, who is convinced that Harrington was not interested in the realities of an agrarian political economy, believes that it didn't occur to him that the exchange of goods and services on an agrarian basis could be studied to determine their laws or in relation to political power. It isn't that Harrington was ignorant of these matters; he was more concerned with the Machiavellian idea "that in a republic the soldiers must be citizens and the citizens soldiers; if the soldiers follow private men for reward, then the republic cannot survive." Harrington's pursuit of his ideal caused him to seek to discover what keeps a soldier alive and what causes the soldier to fight well, and he found this reason in land, which produces both food and money, and in the ownership of land, which provides the citizen with a selfish interest to defend. "It is important—in view of what eminent authorities have said—to realize that Harrington had no concept of economic society as an aspect of human life possessing laws of its own, and therefore none of economic history as the evolution of economic relationships according to a logic of their own."[15] Harrington was reflecting upon the system of medieval military tenures and trying to determine what had happened to England when the system was brought to an end.

The only economic system of which Harrington seemed to be ful-

ly aware was the precapitalist one of master and servant, not one of
investors and wage laborers, the leading actors on the capitalist
stage. The element of control, explicit and implicit, throughout
Harrington's treatment of usury, rents, land ownership, and trade
are mercantilist in one sense, Aristotelian in another, and not completely capitalist. Certainly the expansion of commerce and trade
that is occasionally mentioned by Harrington raise images of the
Tudor policy under Henry VIII and Elizabeth I. Harrington is particularly specific about the role of the state in the control of trade in
Oceana; he was not a nineteenth century free trade advocate with
an optimistic and doctrinaire belief in its efficacy. The solutions
contained in his concept of economic expansion in regard to the
problems of "overplus" are the natural reactions of the luxurious
and fevered city of Plato. In Harrington, however, these reactions
are admired for their naturalness; they are not criticized for their inability to satisfy the demon appetites that created them and that are
now excited by them.

It is difficult to find in the descriptions we have of seventeenth
century England from either the social historians of our time or
from Harrington's contemporaries a reality upon which Harrington
could have based a capitalist economic theory. Some scholars see
capitalism lurking in the racking of rents and in the revoking of the
old associations of landlord and tenant that finally culminated in
enclosures. Evidence of such development existed in England in
Harrington's time. Harrington would have been aware of the inten-
sification of trade and commerce and of the creation of joint stock
companies, which were a significant departure from the traditional
mode of carrying on business. He would have seen the growth of
the mining industry, the shipyards, the textile industry, and the
government bureaucracy.[16] Whether he could or did see where this
growth was leading is still an unanswered question.

The basic units of production in capitalism, the factory and the
large farm, still did not exist in England. All industry existed on a
scale that, even by early capitalist standards, was very small. The
"putting out" system in which the cottager divided his time
between the fields of the local lord, gentleman, or yeoman and his
own loom or workbench to complete the orders given him by the
merchant from the nearby town was a characteristic of the age. In
this era, agriculture and industry were linked in a manner destroyed
later by the Industrial Revolution. In this time before the factory
system, the most important economic functions were performed, as

they had been since time out of mind, by the family, which was usually headed by the father and was composed of wife, children, and servants who lived under one roof, and by a scattering of wage laborers who lived elsewhere and often in poverty. Within this system a form of capitalism was practiced: investments were made in inventory, land, and other goods; contracts were entered into and some people worked for wages. But these conditions were exceptions to the rule of economic life. Despite the expansion of some kinds of enterprise and of the bureaucracy, the older and usual forms and modes of economic life remained untouched. If Harrington had noted considerable social mobility taking place, he was only observing what had occurred within the traditional arrangement of things in England for generations and not what has come to be equated by us with the advent of the capitalist system. People in seventeenth century England were always getting rich while others slid back into genteel poverty or worse. Not until the enclosures reached a peak in the early eighteenth century and not until the first primitive machines were invented for the textile industry could the shape of things to come be seen with reliability.

Such circumstances are part of the answer given to MacPherson, to Tawney who saw Harrington as the observer and theorist of the rising gentry (essentially bourgeois), to Trevor-Roper who saw him as the theorist for a group of declining gentry, or to those who provide us with a Harrington that is either an historian or a political scientist. Their Harrington is not interested in an economic theory apart from, or prior to, the realm of politics. This Harrington is not a competent observer of economic reality; instead, he relied upon writers who were specifically interested in both economics and social status for his information. He does not even claim to be doing what many have claimed for him. The information he received from reading Seldon, Wilson, and others was accepted uncritically and became part of his theory.

Although this method is understandable in a gentleman given to studious habits with wide interests and without the discipline enforced by a rigorous university training, it raises questions about Harrington's account of the development of the situation that produced the civil war in England. Throughout Harrington's "Preliminaries II," in which the history of England is the main concern, John Seldon's *Titles of Honor* is his sole source. Whether he knew of other books on this subject is not known, but Seldon's concept would have suited Harrington's purpose better than any other. Seldon emphasized the continuity between Saxon and Norman land tenures, and this emphasis permitted Harrington to treat feudalism as though it were a single, uniform system that had been transmitted by the Gothic conquerors of Rome and that was everywhere the same. In England, Harrington's feudalism was well established, therefore, even before the Norman conquest. Since the Norman conquerors quickly became English-Saxon in their interests and loyalties, the conquest had not constituted a break in the Gothic balance. Because of Harrington's reliance on Seldon, he was ignorant of what had transpired in the House of Commons from the Norman Conquest to the time of Elizabeth I; and he missed the rise to power of the group that was to be the backbone of the commonwealth, the small tenants-in-chief who were becoming freeholders.[17]

As in economics, so also is Harrington's view of history. Pocock, in drawing our attention to Harrington's reliance on a single source and to his failure to develop his case as well as he could have, says that he has done so in order "to emphasize his [Harrington's] virtual ignorance of later medieval history and [his] inability to chart the decline of the classical feudalism of the Normans." In this regard, Harrington's inability to relate the parliamentary history of England to his account of the movement of the dialectic and his belief that feudalism was everywhere the same and had remained unchanged in England are proof of the doctrinate origin of his dialectic.

In both history and economics, Harrington depended, therefore, more on the authority of others than on his own observations. He was not especially successful, however, in weighing the authorities he depended upon. His system seems to have been based as much upon deductions from an observed present that was to lead to a logical reconstruction of the past. The source of the power possessed by a present group is noted, and a group in the past that controlled the same or a similar source is deduced to have been the "real" power in the system. Or, if a group in the past is known to have possessed power, it is assumed that its components must, even if evidence is lacking, have been based upon the same source. Since this elastic method can be used to analyze the present in a reverse manner with just as much claim to validity, Harrington's use of history and economics is flawed. From his place in time, it was easy, in reviewing what had happened since the time of Henry VII or since the fall of Rome, to see the footprints of the dialectic in history. At another time—after the rise of industrialism, the spread of capitalism, and the triumph of bourgeois values—it is not difficult to see Harrington as the representative of an emerging class or as a harbinger of our own age.

Harrington lived in a time, however, when the associations that we so glibly describe as the links between bourgeois values, the Industrial Revolution, and capitalist economics did not exist—and perhaps did not have to exist. Capitalism and bourgeois values had been part of European civilization and culture for generations, and they did not depend upon each other for maintenance. Now we are convinced that they do, or for a long time did, require one another. Could Harrington have seen this dependence? The evidence that he did is not convincing; his reliance on others for information indicates that he saw mostly through their eyes, not his own. Could he have imagined it? Most certainly there is a logic in this unity that may be convincing even without empirical proof. This conclusion would mean that the Harrington so often praised as an insightful observer, empiricist, and social scientist may not have existed. We may, perhaps, find answers to these questions in the concluding section of this chapter.

IV   *The New Science of Politics*

Looking back at the rule of the Puritans, John Aubrey observed that, "In those times, to have had an inventive and enquiring Witt, was accounted Affectation, which censure the famous Dr. William Harvey could not escape for his admirable Discover of the Circulation of the Blood."[18] When Harvey's great book, *An Anatomical Disquisition of the Motion of the Heart and Blood in Animals,* appeared in 1628, it did not win the praise of the extreme Puritans; but it was widely admired by that group of intellectuals influenced by the "new learning," and by the cause of empiricism espoused by Francis Bacon in his *Novum Organum,* published in 1620. The great promise of radical empiricism and inductive philosophy seemed, in the work of Harvey, to have been fulfilled.

James Harrington was associated with this group; and, as we have seen, his goal was to introduce to the study of politics the same method of analysis that had produced such remarkable results for Harvey. The discoveries yielded by this method would place politics on a sound scientific basis, beyond dispute and passion for the first

time in history. Harrington associated his efforts with those of
Harvey in three ways: he claimed that his method and that of
Harvey were the same and that both were in conformity with the
ideal of Bacon, a method of investigation that was universal in
application. Just as Harvey had developed his principles out of
nature and not out of particular experience, so Aristotle and Cicero
had developed their principles out of nature and observation. In
Harrington's spirited defense of their classics against the criticism of
Hobbes, he equated the methods used in the writings of these two
theorists with those of Harvey. Harvey examined the results of ex-
periments on human bodies and then generalized on the basis of his
observations. Although Aristotle and Cicero examined particular
states, as Hobbes alleged, and generalized, they did use examples
that were unique and restricted to the ancient world, as Hobbes also
charged, but examples that were linked to all times and places
because they had a common and unchanging nature. In other
words, the commonwealths of the ancient world, so far as essentials
were concerned, were as like other commonwealths as the human
bodies studied by Harvey were like those he didn't study.

The second association made by Harrington of his work with that
of Harvey is that the body politic and the human body belong to
the same class of phenomena. "Certain it is," he wrote, "that the
delivery of a model of government (which either must be of no
effect, or imbrace those muscles, nerves, arterys and bones, which
are necessary to any function of a well-order'd commonwealth) is no
less their political anatomy."[19] As for the law of nature, the method
of discovering it applies to both law and men: ". . . the inevitable
necessity or law of nature, is that which truly appertains to men, to
nations and to human laws. To make any other fundamentals, and
then to build upon them, is to build castles in the air."[20]
Harrington, convinced that the similarity he perceived was all-
inclusive, did not hesitate to use the terminology of anatomy in connection with aspects of his theory. The term "Vena Porta" appears
in the *Oceana*, and the observant scholar that noted that particular
usage speculated that Harrington's addiction to trivial detail was a
conscious effort to duplicate the work of Harvey by acknowledging
the complex subject matter of both anatomy and politics and by fitting his description to it.[21]

The same analogy is the basis for Harrington's equation of the
remedy for human illness with that of the disorder of the political
realm. "As certainly and suddenly as a good state of health dispels

the peevishness and peril of sickness, dos a good state of government the animosity and danger of parties."[22] This extremely useful
technique was for Harrington both flexible and persuasive. Readers
who were at least partly convinced that governments all participate
in a common nature later found themselves partly convinced that
the salient fact that, "A political is like a natural body," could also
be used to argue that, like human beings, political bodies also
differed from one another in appearance and in disposition.

Harrington rounded out his association with Harvey by equating
his discovery with that of Harvey, a contention supported by
Toland in his biography of Harrington. Critics who found fault with
Harrington for having not really produced something new were
scolded by him, "Which is as if he [the critic] had told Dr. Harvey,
that wheras the blood is the life was an opinion as antient as Moses,
and no girl ever prick'd her finger, but knew it must have a course;
he had given the world cause to complain of great disappointment
in not shewing a man to be made of gingerbread, and his veins to
run malmsy."[23]

Such associations with Harvey and Bacon are usually taken as
evidence that Harrington was committed to empiricism and to the
inductive method. There are, however, some instances that create
doubt about the exact quality of his commitment. The criticism of
Hobbes leveled by Harrington produced on many occasions the impression that Harrington was strongly opposed to the use of the
deductive method and to "geometry" or abstract science in politics.
But this opposition, after examination, is ambiguous. The specific
complaint that Harrington makes against Hobbes is his establishing
the eternal principles of government upon self-evidence: to declare
some principles self-evident is to deprive them of real scientific
validity. Harrington agreed with Hobbes that there were eternal
principles of government, but he wanted them to depend upon the
inductive method. Once established, these principles could be
applied to political problems with the deductive method.

Harrington was, in a real sense, committed to the use of both
methods in theory. He accepted as self-evident the principle that
nature was universal and immutable; and from this view he
developed the following sequence: observation of diversity in
nature through the use of reason would yield the eternal principles
of politics; the solution of political problems would then be deduced
from the principles.[24] The universal validity of the first, coupled
with prudence, would be the basis for a healthy political order.

Harrington's inductive method invalidated, so far as he was concerned, the self-evident principles of Hobbes, but his own principles were in accord with those revealed in the Bible. Harrington was equally unwilling to accept the authority of the Bible and the self-evidence of Hobbes' psychological principles unless they could be sustained by the inductive method. Much of Hobbes could not be sustained; nothing in the Bible was unsustained.

The second step in the process—the deduction of solutions from principles—established by Harrington, however, was not a science like mathematics; it was an art. Prudence in the sense of matching a new arrangement of political elements to the foundation was an act of invention. In this statement of methods, Harrington was able both to agree and disagree with Hobbes and to offer a unity where none could ordinarily have been expected to have existed. As Charles Blitzer points out, this unity was accomplished by willful distortion on Harrington's part of the meaning of deduction and its application.[25] Harrington certainly didn't use the deductive method as Hobbes did. In *Politicaster*, Harrington paid his respects to deduction by saying it was the more "honorable" method of arguing because, as he put it, deduction moves from cause to effect while induction moves from effect back to cause. Unlike Hobbes, Harrington believed that what is true in one way will also be true in the other. The truth established by induction, though less honorable, is more demonstrable and can be established to resist challenge. This method is what political order requires.

This important perception, that truth is established by science and applied by art, is completed when Harrington gives the final judgment of whether the two have been aptly joined to the people. The theorist, the legislator, and the people now have been assigned their place and function in politics; and, within this definition, the unity sought by Harrington has been achieved. Political science, to the extent that it applies to political roles, encompasses thinking and acting, or leading and following. The theorist, using the inductive method, has discovered the principle of the balance and the superiority of the equal commonwealth; and the next task was the description of the process of its institution.

For both Harrington and Hobbes the establishment of order was a unique event; for, out of chaos, a stable environment would suddenly come into existence. Once accomplished, both thought the new order might approach immortality. Hobbes embedded this event in the "social contract," an agreement that he deemed to be a logical fiction. It seemed to him to be a plausible explanation, given his mechanistic and egoist concept of human nature, for the origin of the state. Harrington, eschewing the deductive method, looked to history for a record of the agencies that had actually accomplished the construction of a commonwealth. In Machiavelli and in Plutarch he found inspiration in the story of Lycurgus, the lawgiver of Sparta, who epitomized the ideal. After Lycurgus had told his people not to change the laws he had given them, he put aside his office and honors and departed to die alone. Harrington seems, in a dialogue entitled *Valerius and Publicola*, published in late 1659, to have assumed for himself the role of Publicola, whose career in Plutarch is compared with that of Solon. Publicola, who had served Rome as a consul and as a general, died as a much honored restorer of Roman honor and as a self-acknowledged imitator of Solon in his dedication to his city and its reputation.

To Harrington, the sole legislator, a *punctum saliens*, created a political creature in the image of a philosophical creature: ". . . it is [this act] the infusion of the soul or faculties of a man into the body of a multitude."[26] Harrington was convinced after reading history that a commonwealth was blessed if the first legislator was only one man and if the government was constructed in all its parts at the same time. Extraordinary tasks required extraordinary men, and they were rare. The problem with assemblies was that their great strength was in judgment and wise choice, for the task in hand required "invention in reason," a solitary profession. "Let one speak, and the rest judge."[27]

Before the legislator could perform his task, the function of the theorist had to be fulfilled; the eternal principles had to be set out and explained. But Harrington also suggested that the theorist had also to perform at the practical level. When Hobbes defined hell as the truth discovered too late, he gave the practical theorist an important responsibility: to discover the truth in time. Harrington took up this task in *Oceana*.

To Harrington, theorizing about politics became so much more pronounced in times of crisis that theories multiplied as men sought deliverance from their fear and their misery. Bad theory drove out good theory in this situation. Since Harrington, who was aware of this factor, does not always distinguish between theorizing that is worthy and that which is not, his statements have the appearance of contradiction. To Harrington, bad theory always oversimplifies politics and subverts the judgment of the people. Its persuasiveness is often in proportion to its deviation from reality toward simplification. Moreover, such theory comes from groups of men who have selfish interests to serve in the crisis. For example, lawyers, because of their obvious attachment to old and outmoded laws, and clergymen, whose lust for power is only thinly veiled, are always untrustworthy theorists. Popular theory, generated under pressure and based upon ignorance, is the kind that is most susceptible to the urge to oversimplify.

Good theory is dispassionate and disinterested in regard to self. It works with the complexity of politics rather than abolishing or ignoring it, and it is the product of the intelligent mind of the one man who has leisure for reflection. The good theorist is a private, rather than a public (in the political sense), "gentleman." Harrington rejected arguments that theorizing should be left to men who held office; for he felt that such men failed to meet his criterion of disinterestedness and would not have sufficient time for reflection. Harrington—a man with plenty of experience on the periphery of power—met the standard contained in his description of a man capable of developing good theory.

Another functional distinction emerges from a consideration of this topic. Theorizing about politics consists of discovering eternal principles and then of advising others as to what will happen and what will work. Those who receive this advice, the actors in politics, are the sole legislators who create the new order; they are the people who must judge it; they are the rulers who then propose laws pursuant to the new order, and they are the people who must finally approve all laws. The final test of theory is its success in solving problems and its acceptance by the people. Harrington was confident that he had discovered the most important eternal principle, the balance; and he assigned to Oliver Cromwell the role of lawgiver. After Cromwell's death, the responsibility passed to his son Richard; but, when Richard Cromwell resigned, Harrington assumed the responsibility himself; but by that time the opportunity to link the authority of theorist and lawgiver to power and interest in any real way was impossible. But, as we shall see, Harrington never relinquished his claim to the title of theorist, nor did he cease, as long as he was able, to explain and advise.

Harrington's reputation as an empiricist and as an inductive theorist depends upon the strength of his commitment to the empirical world as the ground of reality and to induction as the method for knowing and understanding it. In this regard, his emphasis and priority are clear; he was influenced by Bacon, and he anticipates Locke by making empiricism the test of all kinds of truth. His claims for the universality of the inductive method duplicate those made by modern empiricists. We note, however, that he professed admiration for the deductive method on several occasions; he asserted its validity in mathematics, and he began his work by accepting at least one self-evident principle governing nature. We may say that his empiricism was not an absolute reduction of all reality to that single level of existence. His science of politics, rather than rejecting deduction, relegates it to a second and subsidiary position.

We must also ask whether the empirical data upon which Harrington based his theories was accurate, whether he had developed critical tools for sorting the evidence in a manner that is consistent and scientific. His own observations were not always accurate (*cf.* Venice); and he depended upon others, even in regard to conditions in contemporary England. His choice of historians and their observations was, in Blitzer's opinion, artistic rather than scientific and critical. He was led by this method to occasional omissions, as well as to factual errors, in his historical accounts and to faulty descriptions of what was transpiring in England. Although much of this error can be excused by the then rather primitive level of development in the field of statistics, Harrington did not always trouble himself to find the best material available.

In conclusion, we may say that James Harrington, by reading history and the Classics with a sharp eye for whatever in them was presented as factual, especially in regard to feudal tenures, legal obligation, land distribution, and political institutions, saw something that had gone unnoticed before. For instance, just as he read the Bible as history rather than as the revealed word of God, it was just as untoward for him to read Aristotle as a political economist instead of as a philosopher in search of the *summum bonum*. With him, empiricism was not set up in opposition to abstract reasoning, history was not going to supplant philosophy, nor interest replace reason: they were to be combined and strengthened. Harrington appears as something fresh in history and politics because his outlook is empirical, not because he himself was an empiricist. And this distinction is important.

CHAPTER 5

The New Order in England and America

JAMES Harrington suffered much for what he believed. Imprisonment and illness reduced him to misery and insanity after the Restoration, and the wave of popular ridicule that greeted the publication of *Oceana* and his efforts on behalf of its programs made him a notorious public figure even before the monarchy's return. "Heyte Lyte, or to-morrow morning I found an Horse-shoe; being an excellent discourse concerning Government, with some sober and practical expedients, modestly propos'd and written by James Harrington" was a typical satire. Another wit, in a reference to Harrington's penchant for travel and comparative government, suggested that "a Levite and an elder be sent to Survey the Government of the Moon."[1] Others proposed sending Harrington to Jamaica, an island that seems to have possessed risible possibilities for Englishmen in the seventeenth century, to try out his ideas.

The reason that *Oceana* provoked these sallies had less to do with the ideas it contained and more to do with its form and style. Harrington, who called it a political romance, cast it in the form of a utopia, a not uncommon method of presentation. This form may have been used in order to avoid either censorship or prosecution for sedition, or its author, aware that his ambitious attempt to anticipate every possibility involved the description of elaborate and sometimes confusing procedures, may have hoped to help his readers over the dull parts with a soupçon of imagination. Poor Harrington—the result of this effort was to convince many of his readers that he should not be taken seriously; for others, usually of the Monarchist faction or other antirepublican groups, his utopia was a ploy used to disguise who knows what traitorous schemes. Harrington was also hindered in his campaign to gain popular support by the staggering intricacy of the methods of the ballot and of indirect election and by the pages of turgid prose that had to be traversed in order to reach an understanding of the process. Even the transfusion of romance and imagination could not make parts of *Oceana* interesting reading. Because Harrington realized this effect, he was more to the point when he wrote pamphlets explaining the essentials of his system; he eliminated romance and imagination for the most part, and he never tried to explain the ballot again.

I *The Constitution of* Oceana

To begin with, *Oceana* contains an extremely thinly veiled description of conditions in England at Harrington's time, an account of England's recent history, and what purports to be the story of the establishment of an immortal commonwealth on English soil.[2] The time is the future, an age in which all that Harrington promises on behalf of an equal commonwealth has come gloriously true. There are two obstacles that must be overcome before the story can truly begin. The first of these obstacles is "Preliminaries I" and "Preliminaries II," which contain Harrington's political principles of the balance and of the equal commonwealth and his working out of the Harringtonian dialectic of history in Europe and in England. The second obstacle, encountered even in the consideration of both "Preliminaries," is the device forced upon Harrington by the form of the utopia: almost no person, place, or group of people is called by a real name. Instead, each bears a fanciful name or title. The pace is slow until the reader can make such identifications as Olphaus Magaletor to Oliver Cromwell, Panopea to Ireland, Panurgus to Henry VII, and Verulamius to Francis Bacon.

After the "Preliminaries" Harrington's narrative stops being history and becomes an imaginative projection. In a section entitled "The Council of Legislators," he describes how, in the face of the rising concern caused by Oceana's constitutional crisis, Megaletor (Cromwell) and the army discover in each other the means to political deliverance. Supported by the army, Megaletor deposes the parliament and has himself declared "Lord Archon or Sole Legislator of Oceana." A council of fifty notables is summoned to study the constitutions of eleven commonwealths: biblical Israel, Athens, Sparta, Carthage; those of the Achaeans, Aetolians and Lycians; Switzerland, Holland, Rome, and Venice. Another council of twelve is sent to sound out the people of Oceana for their opinions and suggestions. A constitutional convention eventually proposes a basic law composed of thirty orders that are presented and discussed in "The Model of the Commonwealth of Oceana," the fourth section of the book.

The basic law of Oceana is Harrington's attempt to fit the essential processes and institutions of an equal commonwealth to the situation in England. The agrarian law, indirect election and the secret ballot, the assembly, the senate and magistracy, the two part legislative process of proposing and resolving, and the rotation in office are cut from English rather than Venetian cloth.

The agrarian law in Oceana would limit the value in revenue of land owned by any one person to two thousand pounds a year. Harrington reached this figure by estimating the total revenue of land in England at ten million pounds a year. He believed that with the balance in the hands of five thousand men, though this allocation would not necessarily be the final one, the group would be too large to organize itself into an oligarchy. In this respect Harrington followed Machiavelli, who believed that, so long as the few with power were still quite numerous, the republic would be preserved because of the diversity that increases with numbers. They simply would lack the organization and cohesion necessary for an oligarchy. Those who presently held land in excess of the limit would be required to divide it among their sons and to leave none more than the limit. Doweries were also limited, but daughters' and widows' inheritance rights were guaranteed within the limits. The same provisions would hold for Panopea (Ireland), but in Marpesia (Scotland) the standard for the value of land held would be reduced to five hundred pounds a year.

Harrington acknowledged that agrarian laws "of all others have ever bin the greatest bugbears," and in his account of the debate in the Council of Legislators his agrarian limitations were challenged on five counts: they were unnecessary, they were dangerous, they were insufficient to prevent monarchy, they would ruin families, and they would destroy industry. As a postcript the critic charged that, given the traditions and the present allocation of land in Oceana, the agrarian could not be established. The lord archon rejected these criticisms. Invoking Machiavelli, Aristotle, and the Bible, he asserted that history had shown that the agrarian was necessary to the health of a commonwealth, that it was safe, and that it would create new interests that would be a firm basis for opposing the restoration of the monarchy.

The effect of the agrarian on industry and families, however, was a more difficult matter. Concerning the ruin of families, the lord archon said that only three hundred families presently held land in excess of the limit and that, while these holdings would be reduced, they would not be ruined. At any rate, the ruin of a mere three hundred weighed little when such ruination was matched against the good of the entire commonwealth. It is clear, as the archon's argument develops, that he also foresaw the abolition of primogeniture. The only arguments that justify breaking the agrarian in order to preserve the ancient tradition are based upon custom and greatness, both of which serve the interests of monarchy. Though breaking up an estate of two thousand pounds a year among five sons seems hard, the alternative—the maintenance of primogeniture—seems harder. "I must confess I marvel how much it coms to pass, that we should use our children as we do our puppy's; take one, lay it in the lap, feed it with every good bit, and drown five: nay yet worse; for as much as the puppys are once drown'd, wheras the children are left perpetually drowning."³

The fear that an agrarian would discourage industry does not seem to be well founded, according to the lord archon. For, although the owning of land would be restricted, the earning of money and the holding of goods would not be limited. The conscious imperial policy of Oceana would also provide the means for men to apply themselves to an activity that might make them rich. The archon concludes his defense of the agrarian with praise for its moral superiority: it would provide more justly for the children of Oceana, and it would remove much of the temptation to marry for money. "The marriage bed will be truly legitimate, and the race of the commonwealth not spurious."⁴

Elections in Oceana were to be indirect and secret, and the formality and ceremony with which they were to be conducted indicates that Harrington intended the process to be impressive and serious. It was crucial that these important choices be carried out honestly and without the slightest hint of selfish interest. The act of voting was performed in public view, and the elections were important occasions upon which all citizens came together and became part of the whole commonwealth. The elections served not only to select those who would govern but also as a symbolic event: the occurrence coupled individual participation with the experiences of community and even perhaps, given the seasonal regularity with which these assemblies were called, with nature itself. Throughout,

Harrington treated this aspect of the commonwealth with an almost religious solemnity, but he also indicated that he realized that others would find the complexity and ceremony ridiculous.

Elections in Oceana were conducted in four stages over a period of three months. The division of the country into ten thousand "Parishes," into a thousand "Hundreds" (one Hundred for each ten Parishes), and into fifty "Tribes" (or one Tribe for each twenty Hundreds), provides the first three stages in the process. The last step is the election of the national legislature. These parishes, hundreds, and tribes were, given Harrington's description of the process of election, apparently nearly equal in population; and his specificity in describing the surveying of them indicates that they were also comparable in size. Because each succeeding election at the next highest level insured that those who are candidates would be from the level immediately below, there is a guarantee that each geographic region would eventually be represented in the national government.

Not every person would be represented, however, since the right to participate was not granted to women, servants (those who are not economically self-sufficient), and those who fall into the category of "Youths." Youths are males from eighteen to thirty years of age; those over thirty are termed "Elders," and members of this group are divided into two groups. Those with an annual revenue of land, money, or goods of one hundred pounds or more make up the "Horse"; those with less are the "Foot." These two classes would not be equally represented in Oceana's government.

Elections in the parishes were to be held annually on the morning of the first Monday in January at the parish church with all the elders of the place in attendance. When one-fifth of these are selected as deputies to the meeting of the hundred, the method of selection is interesting. A "Proposer" is chosen by lot; the proposer then offers the names of elders for consideration; the elders, by secret ballot, vote either negatively or affirmatively on each name. When the requisite one-fifth has been elected, the process is over. The list of those elected is arranged with members of the horse at the top in order of preference, and those of the foot beneath, again in order of preference. The first five, usually members of the horse, are local parish officials as well as deputies to the hundred. The first two are parish overseers; the next is constable; the last two are church wardens. Elders so elected serve for one year and may be elected again only after two more years have passed. This is the rotation that Harrington believed is so important to the preservation of a commonwealth.

Elections in the one thousand hundreds would take place a month later on the first Monday in February at the "Rendezvous of the Hundred." Deputies from the ten parishes elect not only a justice of the peace, a juryman, a captain of the hundred, and an ensign from the horse but also a juryman, a coroner, and a high constable from the foot. At this level, the election takes place in two steps. After the first nominations have been made and approved, the deputies elect the officials from the list of nominees.

The fifty tribes assemble at the "Rendevous of the Tribe" on the first Monday of March for the next election. The deputies from the two hundred parishes that compose the tribe elect a lord high sheriff, a lord lieutenant, a lord custos rotulorum, a conductor, and two censors. The next day, when elections to national offices would take place, the deputies from the parishes elect five men from the horse; two of these represent the tribe in the upper house of the national legislature; three serve in the lower house, where they are joined by four men chosen from the foot. This process would result in the election of one hundred men to the upper house and three hundred fifty men to the lower house. At each level, to this point, all elected officials serve for only one year and cannot succeed themselves; but representatives to the national legislature serve three year terms and only one-third are elected in any single year. This system of terms is a second application of rotation.

Harrington's system of elections confirms his bias in favor of natural aristocracy of the sort acknowledged in the Classics of which he was so fond. The electors of Oceana could not have constituted a great percentage of the total population, and the office holders were to be drawn from an even smaller class of men. Since the natural aristocrats in Harrington's society would almost always have a disposable income of one hundred pounds a year, this requirement favored the interest that he thought was the basis of power in any society—riches in land, money, and goods. To Harrington, elections that did not provide for the orderly victory of riches were only preparing the ground for sedition. By uniting the natural aristocrats, who were usually recognized by their fellows in a fair election, with the possession of property, Harrington created a practical method of integrating authority and power, a promise we noted much earlier in *Oceana*.

The legislature in the commonwealth of Oceana was composed of two houses; the upper house, or Senate, was composed of three hundred knights from the horse; the lower house, the Prerogative Tribe, had one thousand fifty deputies, four hundred fifty from the horse and six hundred from the foot. One-third of each body was elected annually for three year terms to insure that no group would have power so long that they would abuse it, but each year at least two-thirds of each house would have had experience in their work. In an application of the distinction between proposing and debating on one hand and resolving on the other, which Harrington felt was the method that would finally accomplish the harmony of authority and power, he gave the proposal and debate functions to the Senate and the resolution to the Prerogative Tribe. When the proposed legislation appeared for discussion and debate in the Senate, it could approve, disapprove, or express no opinion. If a majority approved a measure, it was styled a decree of the Senate. There are two kinds of decrees: those that are merely pursuant to laws already in existence; and those that are a matter of new law, an amendment of old laws, or one that concerns law and taxes. The first kind of decree of the Senate is binding without further action; the second must be sent to the Prerogative Tribe.

The Prerogative Tribe, without debate or discussion either in or out of its chamber, may either approve, disapprove, or indicate no opinion. There is no prohibition of the discussion of a proposal by a delegate with his constituents. When the last two alternatives—disapproval or no opinion—received majority support, the result was the proposal's demise or postponement. Approval results in the enactment of a new law. If such a distinction were possible to maintain, it would produce a new breed of politics, a politics without parties and factions, but with willful noncommunication. Harrington considered both political factions and debate among people not qualified to understand the complexity of politics to be dangerous in a commonwealth. Such debate, he believed, invariably led to factionalism.

The executive function of the Oceanic government, the magistracy, was elected by the Senate from its own members. These elections were usually made from among knights that represented each of three groups—that composed of knights in their first year of service, that composed of knights in their second year of service, and that composed of knights in their last year of service. Four annual magistrates were elected by majority vote from any group, and two triennial magistrates were elected from the group of first year knights. The annual magistrates become the lord strategos, president of the Senate and general of the armies, the lord orator, and the first and second censors. The triennial magistrates were the third commissioners of the seal and of the treasury. Three councils of the commonwealth, state, religion, and trade were also elected. One-third of the membership of each—five, four, and four, respectively—were chosen each year from the group of first year knights. The Senate also chose ambassadors and, in emergencies, the dictator.

The functions of these magistrates are not at all mysterious. Foreign affairs is the responsibility of the Council of State and its subcommittee, the Council of War, which may operate in secret and which is only indirectly responsible to the Senate. The Council of Trade, which has the power to enforce a mercantilist policy in regard to commerce, is directed to study the effect of foreign trade on the economic health of the country and to regulate it accordingly. The Council of Religion controlled all aspects of religion in the state with the purpose of insuring freedom of conscience. It was to administer the universities, oversee the established church, and regulate the education and conduct of its clergy. The commissioners of the seal and the treasury served as judges of chancery and of the exchequer and, with the lord strategos, composed the signory. The signory seems to have been Harrington's executive in Oceana, for this body has the broadest grant of power in times of peace. Nevertheless, it is not a strong executive body. It is not organized under anyone's leadership, nor on the basis of any party or principle. Its membership is composed of individuals elected and changed each year. It lacks, for these reasons, both coherence and continuity.

Of major interest is the method used to govern Oceana in wartime or in emergency. Machiavelli's *Discourses* contained praise for the wisdom of making provision for dictatorial efficiency when the commonwealth is in danger. Harrington apparently agreed, for his Oceana is provided with a short-term dictator to cope with such situations. Whenever the Senate considered doing so necessary, it could increase the size of the Council of War by adding nine knights to its membership; and this group became the dictator. It could serve for three months and could pass laws that would remain in effect for up to a year if not repealed by the Senate and the Prerogative Tribe.

Charles Blitzer, in his evaluation of the government of Oceana, remarks upon an important and curious aspect of it; there is, despite the high level of political activity, almost no bureaucracy in Oceana.[5] So far as can be determined, Harrington, often precise and detailed to the point of prolixity, provides his commonwealth with only twenty-four bureaucrats. Either Harrington believed that such bureaucracy was not part of what should be considered politics (he could not have been unaware of its growth and importance in Tudor and Stuart England) or else, without engaging in explicit criticism, he may have felt that such a bureaucracy was dangerous and unnecessary in a commonwealth. The amount of decentralization he specified for two very important government functions—tax collecting, and the raising and maintaining of an army—indicate that he may have felt that a "king-sized" bureaucracy was unnecessary. Expenditures and revenues were to be set by the national legislature, but the collecting and setting of taxes was a function of the tribe, the hundred, and the parish. Troop levies were also farmed out to these organs of local government.

Local government officials at the parish level in Oceana were generally responsible for keeping records, running the frequent elections, maintaining the peace, and collecting taxes. The responsibilities were not much different in the hundred except that courts had to be maintained and that the militia had to be assembled and drilled. The tribe had these responsibilities, as well as the task of maintaining communications with the national government. With some variations, the capital of Oceana, Emporium (London), conforms with this pattern of local government. As the rural area retained much of the same structure that had existed before the civil war, so did the commonwealth's chief city.

Education and military training, both of which directly affected citizens classed as youth by Harrington, were treated together in the *Oceana;* and this association was a logical one for a man who was familiar with Plato and Aristotle. Education and military training were each compulsory to an extent that was exceptional for the time and both were matched to the requirements of the individual and of the commonwealth. The administration of the educational system was the responsibility of the Council of Religion, for it made all appointments to the universities at which ministers of the church were trained. "An ounce of wisdom," Harrington said, "Is worth a pound of clergy."[6] The first and second censors were chancellors of the two major universities, Clio and Calliope (Oxford and Cambridge), as well as presidents of the Councils of Religion and Magistracies.

With the exception of the first-born son, which either may or may not be educated (it is the parents' choice), all male children must be sent to school when they are nine and continue their education until they are fifteen. At that time parents must choose either to apprentice their son or to send him on for more schooling. Since even the poor are to obey this regulation, each tribe must provide publicly supported school for all. At either eighteen or twenty-three years of age, every young man must begin to serve the commonwealth in the army. Some young men will be permitted to travel abroad, but this will be regulated by an application procedure. Those who do travel must write a paper about what they have learned.

With the notable exception of lawyers, clergymen, and doctors, who begin their practices at age eighteen, as well as of first-born sons, all young men have a military obligation. The term of service was for one year, but no one served for two years in a row. Those who refuse service pay heavily by forfeiting twenty percent of their wealth for the protection others afford them and by being barred from holding public office. Harrington's army is a citizen army because of the ideas of Machiavelli. Since mercenary armies, in the opinion of both Machiavelli and Harrington, were unreliable and usually dispirited fighters, a commonwealth would best be defended if the hand that held the sword also drove the plow on land owned by the plowman.

Harrington's army is also large by the standards of his day. "To make wars with small force is no husbandry, but a wast, a disease, a lingering and painful consumtion of men and mony. . . ."[7] Each year in February the entire youth of Oceana was to assemble for the organization and training of an army. Those eligible were divided by lot and ballot into the standing army, the army of occupation, or the militia. The standing army was assembled twice a year for games and drill and was to be ready for combat at any time. Officers were elected by all the men, who were themselves divided into horse and foot depending upon their ability to pay for their equipage. The elders of Oceana were organized into garrison forces, and their mission was to defend their estates against invading forces. The entire armed forces would serve in wartime under the direction of the lord strategos and other officers selected by the national government.

Because Harrington wrote about the commonwealth of Oceana some years after its founding, he was also able to say something about the imaginary success of his brainchild. We are told that the extremely light tax burden in Oceana had produced, in the period of prosperity and plenty that followed its establishment, surplus revenues that were so wisely invested that, after twenty-one years, the excise tax could be abolished. The absence of a bureaucracy, and a large, though inexpensive, army, probably lent assistance to this success. The population, which had increased beyond all expectations, provided additional opportunities for national greatness. Because of all this, the name of the lawgiver was held sacred—"His Name is as Precious Ointment"—and various honors were heaped upon him.[8]

Harrington's *Oceana* is not like Plato's *Republic*, "a design laid up in the sky," that is to be used as a standard for judging all existing governments. Nor is it like Butler's *Erewhon* or More's *Utopia*, both of which are "nowhere." *Oceana* is a practical utopia and resembles Plato's *Laws* in its intention. Harrington definitely wanted it built in England and even expected it to be built. It was not, we shall see, given the reception Harrington had hoped for. Despite all the discussion and attention it did receive, it remained, during its author's lifetime, an imaginary realm in the popular mind that differed little from other impractical Utopias.

II   A Life at Odds

Harrington's defense and advocacy of his ideas became, after the *Oceana* appeared, inseparable from his life. From the winter of 1656 until his arrest and imprisonment in December 1661, he was an active pamphleteer, an articulate member of a political faction, and the organizer and presiding officer of an experimental and educational political club, The Rota. Throughout this period, however, Harrington preserved his standing as a "private," as opposed to "public," person. He held no official position, nor did he actively seek one. Though passionately involved in politics, he remained an amateur.

We have already examined the controversies that involved Harrington in the defense of his theory of the balance and his belief in the superiority of the equal commonwealth and of the political circumstances that surrounded them. Members of the clergy, intellectuals from the university, and Royalists of other professions were his opponents in these disputes. Harrington also found himself arguing with his fellow Republicans and with the Fifth Monarchy men, fanatics who believed that the Second Coming of Christ was at hand.

Henry Stubbe, a convinced Republican and an able supporter of Harrington, was his master's target in two short pamphlets, *A Letter unto Mr. Stubs* and *A Sufficient Answer to Mr. Stubs*.[9] Both of these appeared in 1659, one in the late winter, the other in the fall; and both took issue with the proposals made by Stubbe that implied criticism of Harrington's design for an equal commonwealth. These attacks on Stubbe may also have been directed at other Republicans aligned with him, especially his friend Sir Henry Vane, the Younger, and John Milton, both of whom were Republicans with a Puritan flavor. Stubbe, who thought that Harrington was wrong in thinking that an equal commonwealth would immediately be strong enough to resist a Stuart restoration, argued that people were not convinced that a commonwealth was in their interest, that they believed a faction or elite would initially have to govern without the consent of all; and that they thought that all could not be granted full right of participation. Some protection against sedition would have to be created. Harrington replied that Stubbe was advocating an oligarchy and that such a commonwealth would deviate so much from its Classical models that it would fail in its purpose.

In *A Parallel of the Spirit of the People, with the Spirit of Mr. Rogers*, Harrington responded to criticisms of his various constitutional proposals that had been made by the foremost writer in the group of many Fifth Monarchy Men, John Rogers.[10] Rogers was remarkable because, although he shared many of the millenarian principles of the "Saints," he was a moderate and essentially reasonable man whose arguments and positions on political issues were democratic. His advocacy of theocratic government or rule by the "Saints," was open rather than narrow and restrictive. That anyone opposed to tyranny would be permitted to join the "Saints" in a coalition government was viewed by Rogers as a compromise between Harrington's proposal to extend the right to participate to members of all factions and the extreme Fifth Monarchy position which restricted participation to the "Saints." Harrington argued that the spirit of the people was determined by interest alone and not by such extraneous factors as loyalty, reason, tradition, and faith. If the interests of the citizens were against monarchy and sedition, the people would oppose them. Since such interest existed, Harrington thought, it was the basis of his unwillingness to water down his concept of citizenship and participation in a commonwealth.

More of Harrington's writing during 1659 was aimed at popularizing and explaining the necessity of England's having a commonwealth and the advisability of that commonwealth's being equal. These pamphlets, which were often commentaries on conditions in England, contained analyses of institutions and the potential that they held for either good or evil in reference to the equal commonwealth. If there is any development shown in these writings, it is Harrington's tendency to state his ideas more briefly and more forcefully. Perhaps less obviously, some of the pamphlets indicate that Harrington's urgency is also a product of his declining confidence in the ability of the people to see in which direction their real interests lay. By the late fall of that year, in *Valerius and Publicola*, Harrington confessed his disappointment in the people; and we can sense that Harrington assumed the double role of lawgiver and suffering servant to his country because of the failure of the Cromwells to establish a commonwealth, the increasing sentiment in favor of restoration, and the impotence of the commonwealth faction in Parliament. The accomplishment of a commonwealth, though still an historical necessity for England and inevitable, was now placed by Harrington beyond its present historical context and became the destiny of England instead of its very next step.

Harrington's most overt political activity consisted of his close cooperation with the small group of commonwealthmen that had been elected to the Parliament that met in January 1659. Approximately fifty of the members of this body were in favor of some kind of commonwealth, and ten of these supporters constituted a faction that, under the leadership of Henry Nevill, was committed to Harrington's proposals. Initially, this group supported and appealed to Richard Cromwell as the potential lawgiver; and it also advocated the creation of an upper house of Parliament that was to serve the purpose of the Harringtonian senate and that was to be constituted in a like manner.

Richard Cromwell resisted the appeals of the commonwealthmen and sent Parliament home in April 1659. Within two weeks, Richard Cromwell was gone, and the Long Parliament was back. Harrington's pamphleteering increased, but he joined in presenting a "humble petition" to the Parliament that proposed a committee composed of one hundred and three men who were to be drawn from every section of republican opinion to study the ways by which such a government could be established. Many of Harrington's friends and adversaries were included on this committee, and the proposal received a polite reception, but the petition failed in its objective and was never seriously considered.[11]

Harrington gained his greatest success and was most seriously considered in London's coffeehouses by the intellectual and slightly bohemian society that flourished in them. After *Oceana* first appeared in 1656, the book and its ideas and proposals became the subjects for debate and discussion among men of this milieu. This kind of comment grew and became a stable element in the intellectual life of London. During the fall of 1659, Harrington was moved by this current interest in his ideas and by the potential for publicity to formally organize a club, The Rota, to test the mechanism of the Venetian ballot and to debate important political issues. Both Samuel Pepys and John Aubrey wrote descriptions of the meetings of The Rota and of the people who attended.[12]

Times were most uneasy in late 1659 and in early 1660, and London was a city of rumors. It may have been inevitable in the midst of the uncertainty and vacillation of the Long Parliament that the Stuarts would return, but Harrington and his friends resisted that pessimistic conclusion. The Rota met almost every night during this period, and the attendance was good. Aubrey was at his most interesting, and most brief, when he wrote that ". . . he had every night a meeting at the (then) Turke's head, in the New Pallace-yard, where was made purposely a large ovall-table, with a passage in the middle for Miles to deliver his Coffee. About it sate his Disciples, and the Virtuosi. The Discourses in this Kind were the most ingeniose, and smart, that ever I heard, or expect to heare, and bandied with great eagerness: the Arguments in the Parliament howse were but flatt to it."[13] There was a ballot box at these meetings, and after each debate those in attendance would vote. "One time Mr. Stafford and his Gang came in, in drink, from the Taverne and affronted the Junto (Mr. Stafford tore their Orders and Minutes). The Soldiers offer'd to kick them downe stayres, but Mr. Harrington's moderation and persuasion hindered it." Aubrey remarked that the whole process was interesting and many thought that, with the king's return an impossibility, the methods of The Rota might be a way of settling England's political problems.

In Feburary 1660, dissatisfied with the Long Parliament's well-demonstrated inability, General Monk and the army took matters into their own hands. The Rota immediately suffered a drop in attendance; and its proceedings, without a crowd and with the outcome of the crisis less and less in doubt, were dreary and sad. On

February 20, 1660, when Samuel Pepys and a friend attended what was to be the last meeting of The Rota, the debate concerned the question of whether learned or unlearned subjects were best. The answer was apparently so inconclusive that Pepys did not record the vote: "After a small debate upon the question . . . the Club broke up very poorly, and I do not think they will meet anymore."[14] On this occasion Harrington essayed one last prediction: "Well, the King will come in. Let him come-in, and call a Parliament of the greatest Cavaliers in England, so they be men of estates, and let them but sett seven years, and they will all turn Commonwealthe's men."[15] To Harrington, interest and the balance would win.

Two of Harrington's last pamphlets, *The Ways and Means Whereby an Equal and Lasting Commonwealth May be Suddenly Introduced* and *The Rota*, represent a considerable scaling down of his program.[16] Both concentrated on the consensus favoring a freely elected Parliament that would not be an equal commonwealth but would serve as the first step toward the construction of one. These hopes were balanced, however, by Harrington's acknowledgment that popular support for the monarchy was growing stronger and by his willingness to acquiese to the Restoration if that was what the people wanted. One last brief work, *A Word Concerning a House of Peers*, appeared in February 1660, and Harrington argued that, even if it could be established, a monarchy would not be a practical solution to England's constitutional problems. A commonwealth would still come about by one of two methods, ". . . the one quicker, the other slower: the quicker way will be by the workmen, the slower by the work."[17] Harrington also attacked the institution of a House of Peers. Such a body would be the death of the liberty of conscience because it would depend upon the king and would include ". . . divines, who (for the greater part) are no fair huntsmen, but love dearly to be poaching or clubbing with the secular arm. . . ." Ultimately, only a House of Commons would be able to rule. Even with the generals serving as peers, the army would have to depend upon the people who controlled the means to feed it—the landowners, the commons.

When Charles II returned to England on the coattails of General Monk, James Harrington ceased his efforts and retired once more to his study. In an atmosphere of quiet and reflection he met with old friends and discussed old issues; he was seemingly content to be divorced from the politics of the Restoration and to consider politics as a study again. He was, unfortunately, a marked man; the uneasy monarchy, so recently the victim of plots and hostile theories, could not let Harrington leave the politics of action so easily.

Harrington was not only the most prominent living Republican and a man who had commanded an impressive following, but also the cousin of another James Harrington who had served Cromwell ably and in important ways. The family connection and the confusion over the similarity of names probably heightened the suspicion surrounding Harrington and his intentions. When some time had passed and Harrington had made no hostile move against the king, a man was sent to entrap him. He asked Harrington to write some advice to the king on how to rule so as to prevent a recurrence of the civil war. Though Harrington was working on his *System of Politics*, which was published posthumously, he complied with the request and was arrested for his troubles in November 1661.

He was first taken to the Tower of London, where he was confined and examined by a committee of Royalists, Lord Lauderdale, Sir George Carteret, and Sir Edward Walker. The object of the investigation was to link Harrington with the eminent plotter, John Wildman, and with various subversive activities that had been reported. Harrington resisted these attempts and protested his innocence throughout the interview. He did, however, confess to being "eminent in Principles contrary to the King's government, and the Laws of this Nation," but he maintained that this contrariness could be found in his writings, not in his actions. Upon this distinction, between expression and action, between private and public activities, Harrington placed his case for freedom. This argument did not convince his examiners, who accepted his distinctions as legitimate, but were not convinced that he had maintained this separation in his own life.[18]

Harrington remained in the Tower until April 23, 1662, when he was moved to a prison on St. Nicholas Island in order to avoid complying with a writ of habeas corpus obtained by his sisters. At this new prison Harrington was so badly treated that his health suffered. A bond was posted by his brother, and Harrington was permitted to leave prison and live under guard in Plymouth. These conditions were somewhat more pleasant, and he received medical treatment for his illness. His scurvy, a disease often contracted in jails at the time, was treated by an incompetent physician, however, and the medicine caused some brain damage. This tragedy moved the government to finally release Harrington to the care of his sisters.

When Harrington returned to his home in London, the extent of the damage became clearer:

> . . . but he grew to have a phansy that his Perspiration turned to Flies and sometimes to Bees; and he had a versatile timber house built in Mr. Hart's garden (opposite to St. James's Parke) to try the experiment. He would turne it to the sun, and sitt towards it; then he had his foxtailes there to chase away and massacre all the Flies and Bees that were to be found there, and then shut his Chasses [window]. Now this experiment was only to be tryed in Warme weather, and some flies would lie so close in the cranies and cloath (with which it was hung) that they did not presently shew themselves. A quarter of an hower after perhaps, a fly or two, or more, might be drawen-out of the lurking holes by the warmeth; and then he would cry out, Doe not you see it apparently that these come from me.[19]

On many other matters, it is reported, his conversation indicated that he retained his old intelligence and wit.

Aside from *The Mechanics of Nature*, a pamphlet in which he attempted to counter the diagnosis of insanity that had been made by his doctors, Harrington wrote no more.[20] He lived in the pleasant company of his friends; and he finally married a childhood sweetheart, the daughter of Sir Marmaduke Dorrel, who had apparently refused him many times when they had been younger. Theirs was not a love match, and Toland ungallantly remarked that "An action that will better persuade the world he was not truly himself, was his marrying in this condition."[21] In addition to his mental distemper Harrington came to suffer from gout; during the last year of his life, he was palsied. He died September 11, 1677, in an England that was not yet an equal commonwealth and at the end of a life that had been filled with a variety of experience and creativity.

III   *Harrington's Influence*

From the beginning, thinking and acting in politics have been twined with influence. It is influence that has moved people to accomplish great deeds that stand in history and memory. The Greeks, the first political actors in the Western World, realized and acted upon the connection—influence, accomplishment, immortality—and made it the central concern of their preoccupation with public life. James Harrington's career moved along the path of this same development; for, after trying, and failing, to gain the influence in English politics that would have erected the immortal commonwealth that would have been his own memorial, he contented himself with the belief that where theories and ideas had not been sufficient to his immediate purpose, history would serve his ultimate purpose. These purposes were, after all, one and the same: a political order fitted not only to human nature but to the specific historical context. The perfect example of political science and political art was inevitable, now or later, and forever.

When the plan for an equal English commonwealth began to dissolve, Harrington wrote, the cry of the prophet without honor in his own country or in his own time: "If this Age fails me, the next will do me Justice."[22] To measure influence accurately is difficult. In the present, our view is skewed, foreshortened, and tends to magnify every fact. Looking back eliminates these problems and presents us with others. Ideas have a life of their own and often appear in history separated from their originators. To tell people who believe that property determines power that they have been influenced by James Harrington might come as a mild surprise to them. Ideas become part of the climate of opinion and are often beyond question or challenge, unexamined prejudices. This was the fate of much of what Harrington either originated or took from others and made part of his *Oceana*. Later, many constitution writers, legislators, and political reformers helped themselves to Harringtonian theories and devices without realizing that they were in his debt. In such instances, his influence must be regarded as subtle or indirect.

Other individuals and groups, however, have been so explicit that they invoked Harrington as an authority in their applications of his ideas. Since the decade of the 1670s, there have been three separate traditions in political theory that can be directly traced to James Harrington. These are the Whig tradition in England; the basic principles and political institutions of the United States; and the continental, especially French, attachment to rationally drawn, written constitutions of complicated design.

At the end of Harrington's life, his ideas were carried forward by a group of intellectuals and parliamentary backbenchers who are considered by J. G. A. Pocock as "neo-Harringtonians." These included Henry Nevile, Andrew Fletcher, Walter Moyle, John Toland, Robert Viscount Molesworth, John Trenchard, and Thomas Gordon.[23] Like most of Harrington's disciples, they were not committed to all of his ideas and devices. Harrington's writings contain so many bits and pieces from the Classics and from other systems of government that almost no one either accepts or rejects all of them. The neo-Harringtonians were opposed to all that smacked of royal power and political centralization. They usually represented country constituencies or had strong links with the gentry that Harrington thought was rising and that his critic, H. R. Trevor-Roper, believes was declining. If Harrington was concerned about the triumph of principle, his followers were much more interested in the victory of a particular interest. Their program was generally negative; they opposed the excise tax, the standing army, the growth of the central bureaucracy, and the existence of a public debt. Most of the active politicians in this group served in the House of Commons, and their primary targets were members of their own house who held governmental offices and depended upon the king's favor and those members of the House of Lords that served the monarchy's interests rather than those of the nation at large. The most obvious legacy of Harrington for this faction was the relationship of land to power, the close identification of citizenship with military service and the practice of government.

There were deviations, however, from Harrington's evaluation of English government prior to the civil war. Although Harrington was critical of what he called the Gothic balance, the neo-Harringtonians praised it inordinately and regarded it as a golden age of mixed government very much like that praised as best by Polybius. What Harrington saw as confusion and strife, the neo-Harringtonians thought was a healthy balance among commons, lords, and king, the mixed constitution of a happy commonwealth. Those aspects of later Stuart policy that they opposed were condemned as destructive of this productive system of checks and balances.

After the 1690s, this Whig tradition became more dependent upon and was influenced by the political philosophy of John Locke. Not only did Locke continue the Harringtonian emphasis upon property and the assertion of popular rights against royal government, but he provided a more fully developed theory of interest based upon a strictly empirical psychology. Locke was a philosopher as well as a theorist, and those Whigs who read him were able to assimilate what he and Harrington had written quite easily. Locke was, after all, far more successful in a worldly sense, and for that reason he was considered more respectable than Harrington. By the time Locke wrote, the principle of popular government had triumphed in the Glorious Revolution of 1688, and the land-owning gentry were truly on the verge of realizing the power that Harrington had prematurely conferred upon them a generation earlier.

During the eighteenth century, this Whig tradition divided into two sections. In England, it continued in Parliament to be the ideology of one of the two great political factions. In intellectual circles, after undergoing some changes, the tradition emerged as utilitarianism and philosophical radicalism under the leadership of Jeremy Bentham, who all but ignored Harrington's contribution. The importance of history was denied, and the basis for public policy was interest alone. When Bentham's ideas stimulated the movement for reform in the early nineteenth century, Harrington was no more than a footnote, although several of the reforms proposed for Parliament bore his imprint, especially the call for frequent elections. When the reformers and liberals of that century looked back in history for their origins, they went no farther than Locke and the generation of 1688.

The other half of the Whig tradition, which retained a faith in republican institutions, was exported to the New World, where the Harringtonian element was preserved and written into the Constitution of the United States and, before that, into the constitutions of the various states and colonies. H. F. Russell-Smith, the foremost commentator on Harrington's influence in America, has written:

The written constitution, the unlimited extension of the elective principle, and the separation of the three functions of government lie at the root of American political theory; the equal division of property among the children is one of the most far reaching social and political factors in the United States; the principle of indirect election, though now discredited, has been employed since the formation of the Union. Short tenure of power, the multiplication of offices, the system of checks and balances, rotation, the ballot, the use of petitions, the popular ratification of constitutional legislation, the special machinery for guarding the constitution, religious liberty, popular education—all these things play their part in America.[24]

This list is considerable, but the reasons for its ideas that are advanced do not always make *Oceana* and Harrington the origin of them. By the time the United States Constitution was written and the character of American social and intellectual life had developed, the stream that had risen with Harrington was being fed, and muddied, by many others. A closer and more direct relationship can be established between Harrington and the various colonial constitutions drawn up in the seventeenth century and, later, the constitution of the commonwealth of Massachusetts.

Three colonies, Carolina, New Jersey, and Pennsylvania, were settled during the period 1660 - 1690; and in each an attempt was made to create a Harringtonian commonwealth. Two constitutions in Carolina had the balance and the complex system of indirect election embedded in them, but both concepts proved to be too unwieldy for the colonists. By 1700, the constitution of Carolina had been changed so much that it no longer bore any resemblance to its ideal.[25]

The colonial constitution of New Jersey, drawn up in 1683, was most Harringtonian. It consisted of a governor, governor's council, and a grand council. Membership in the grand council rotated, and the balance of interests and property was guaranteed. William Penn, the founder of Pennsylvania, had become familiar with Harringtonian ideas at Oxford in the early 1660s. Although the constitution he wrote for his colony contained the ballot, rotation, and the separation of debate and result, it was a failure and was replaced almost at once.

John Adams, an ardent admirer of Harrington's, and James Otis, his associate, played important roles in the framing of the Massachusetts Constitution. Their devotion to Harringtonian principles was so obvious that, as a jest, someone proposed changing the name of the state from Massachusetts to Oceana during the constitutional convention in 1779. The motion was defeated, but the point of the mover was clear. This attempt and the United States Constitution remain as the most nearly Harringtonian constitutions.[26]

Harrington's works were translated into French as early as 1700, and he was admired as a commonwealthman by Montesquieu. Montesquieu did criticize, however, the concept of liberty that he found in *Oceana*. Nevertheless, *Oceana* came to be acknowledged by French writers as the best English utopia of the civil war period, and by the time of the French Revolution his ideas were current enough to figure prominently in the pamphlet literature of the period. Harrington's foremost proponent was the Abbé Sieyes, who was interested in drawing up a constitution for revolutionary France that would develop in the logical manner of the one contained in *Oceana*. Edmund Burke criticized both Sieyes and Harrington for the artificial and abstract quality of their proposals; and, though the ideas and proposals of both became popular and were much discussed, their impact in France was vitiated by the time of Napoleon.[27]

Posterity has recognized Harrington's contribution to political thought. His method is widely employed, usually without attribution, in the fields of interest group analysis and comparative government. The *Oceana* is widely referred to as a monument of utopian literature. Certain devices, such as the ballot, praised by Harrington, are part of the way disputes are settled. The Harringtonian commonwealth, however, is still "nowhere." If we think we see it in this or that constitution, it is probably because we want to see it, or because we make the mistake of seeing the whole in just a part of whole. Modern republics are imperfect monuments to Harrington's memory, but his immortality rises from the persistence of his ideas and from the shared experiences that produce their reoccurrence.

IV   *An Evaluation*

Original ideas are rare; and, useful or not, their discovery should be celebrated. Harrington's balance, taken together with his description of the equal commonwealth, contains elements of originality and imagination; and his concepts must be given a place among the serious attempts at order in the Western tradition of political theory. His great error is to have claimed too much for the science and art of politics and to have expected far more of England and its people than they could accomplish.

Good intentions, which are not so rare, must at least be credited; for nothing base or selfish existed in Harrington's vision of a new order. We should not be convinced by attempts to link him to an interest or a class on a conscious level. Unlike many others with good intentions, Harrington paid for his errors or misjudgments with his own freedom and health and not with the lives and freedom of others. He was fortunate that his own impulses were not modern in the sense that he would sacrifice his own principles to subject others to tyranny in order to gain victory. He was fortunate, also, to have freed himself from the closed intellectual world of seventeenth century religious warfare. Harrington stands, with only a few others, on the frontier between two tendencies toward arrogance, one derived from theological certainty, the other from secular inspiration such as the dialectic of history, rationalism, science, or empiricism. That he was sure of the truth he had discovered is obvious, but we may be sure, too, that he accepted limits on what could be done to others in the name of that truth. His was an attempt to persuade through argument, not to subjugate through coercion or to mislead by propaganda.

There is, in such a condition, an ineluctable tension; for to be certain, as Harrington was, but to refrain from all-out action is in the best traditions of Humanism, either Christian or secular. There may be, in this aspect of Harrington's character, evidence that the Classical Humanism recovered in his time did not always lead to the destruction of public order, as Hobbes charged, but molded disciplined people with disciplined intellects. The unity Harrington sought as a political theorist, could not, given this acceptance of limits on action, be achieved. Some thinkers or philosophers fail to find this completeness intellectually, but Harrington is not one of these. His failure was his inability to find a world with the regularity and the harmony to match the one that existed in his imagination. In our own age, where Humanism exists devoid of restraint, men have set about creating a new world to match their ideas without any regard for the niceties and civility that were part of Harrington's charm. They create misery instead; and the unity, at last, is the unity of the graveyard.

Harrington suffered the tension implicit in his situation and much else besides. A civilized man in an uncivilized age, his life is an example of how a citizen should behave when the center does not hold. He marshaled wit and imagination on behalf of truth, and he sacrificed himself for it. He did so reluctantly, we should remember, and not in the enthusiastic but boring manner of martyrs. His life came close to satisfying the aesthetic requirements of Humanism.

Harrington deserves our attention. On the strength of the balance, he must be placed in the second rank of political theorists. On the basis of *The Commonwealth of Oceana*, he belongs in the second rank of utopian writers. But more important, perhaps, than either of these, he is a man to study in an unsettled age. His experience reaches out across the years to us. So alike are the crises of the West in his age and in ours that understanding him in his context is a step toward understanding us in ours.

Notes and References

Chapter One

1. It is probably cold comfort for those in pursuit of a single James Harrington, but Sir Isaiah Berlin has isolated twenty-five theories interpreting Machiavelli's *The Prince*. This feat was accomplished in 1964, and the number has increased. Cited in Niccolo Machiavelli, *The Discourses*, ed. Bernard Crick (Baltimore, 1970), p. 15.
2. Charles Blitzer, *An Immortal Commonwealth* (New Haven, 1960), pp. ix - x.
3. Judith N. Shklar, "Ideology Hunting: The Case of James Harrington," *American Political Science Review*, LIII (September 1959), 692.
4. Felix Raab, *The English Face of Machiavelli* (Toronto, 1964), pp. 185 - 87.
5. Shklar, p. 692. The next quotation is from the same page.
6. Thomas Hobbes, *Leviathan*, ed. Michael Oakeshott (Oxford, 1960), p. x.
7. John Toland, "The Life of James Harrington," in James Harrington, *Works: The Oceana and Other Works*, ed. John Toland (1771; rpt. Darmstadt, 1963), p. xv.
8. "The Prerogative of Popular Government," *Works*, p. 272.
9. "Oceana," *Works*, p. 37; S. B. Liljegren, ed., *James Harrington's Oceana* (Heidelberg, 1924), p. 15.
10. "A System of Politics," *Works*, p. 466. The next quotation is from the same work and page.
11. "Oceana," *Works*, p. 37; Liljegren, p. 15.
12. Aristotle, *The Politics*, trans. T. A. Sinclair (Baltimore, 1962), book III, chap. 7, p. 115.
13. Hobbes, p. 121.
14. Aristotle, book III, chap. 9, pp. 119 - 21.
15. "Oceana," *Works*, p. 37; Liljegren, p. 15.
16. "The Art of Lawgiving," *Works*, p. 362.
17. "Oceana," *Works*, p. 69; Liljegren, pp. 54 - 55.
18. "Oceana," *Works*, pp. 37 - 38; Liljegren, p. 15.
19. "Oceana," *Works*, p. 38; Liljegren, p. 16.
20. "Oceana," *Works*, p. 40; Liljegren, p. 18.
21. "Oceana," *Works*, p. 66; Liljegren, p. 51.
22. "The Art of Lawgiving," *Works*, p. 431.
23. "Oceana," *Works*, p. 37; Liljegren, p. 15.

24. Hobbes, p. 115, quoted as it appears in "Oceana," *Works*, p. 38; Liljegren, p. 16. The next quotation is from the same work and page.

25. "Oceana," *Works*, p. 32; Liljegren, p. 10.

26. "Oceana," *Works*, p. 39; Liljegren, p. 17.

27. Niccolo Machiavelli, *The Discourses*, trans. Leslie J. Walker, S. J. (New Haven, 1960), p. 335. This paragraph and the next contain a summary of this chapter of *The Discourses*.

28. "Oceana," *Works*, pp. 39 - 40; Liljegren, p. 17 - 18.

29. "Oceana," *Works*, p. 68; Liljegren, pp. 53 - 54.

30. "Oceana," *Works*, p. 39; Liljegren, p. 17.

31. Aristotle, book V, chap. 2, pp. 192 - 208.

32. "Pian Piano," *Works*, p. 528.

33. "The Prerogative," *Works*, p. 227. The next quotation is from the same work and page.

34. "The Prerogative," *Works*, p. 228.

35. "The Prerogative," *Works*, p. 230.

36. "The Art of Lawgiving," *Works*, p. 364. The next quotation is from the same work and page.

37. R. H. Tawney, "Harrington's Interpretation of His Age," *Proceedings of the British Academy*, XXVII (1941), 17 - 18.

38. Charles Blitzer, ed., *The Political Writings of James Harrington* (New York, 1955), p. xxvii.

39. J. G. A. Pocock, *The Ancient Constitution and the Feudal Law* (New York, 1967), pp. 124 - 47.

40. H. R. Trevor-Roper, *The Gentry 1540 - 1640* (London, n.d.), p. 45.

41. Raab, pp. 201 - 203.

Chapter Two

1. William T. Bluhm, "Naturalistic Political Science as Interest Group Theory: Harrington and Bentley," in *Theories of the Political System* (Englewood Cliffs, New Jersey; 1964), p. 331.

2. Blitzer, *An Immortal Commonwealth*, p. 3.

3. J. G. A. Pocock, "Machiavelli, Harrington, and English Political Ideologies in the Eighteenth Century," *William and Mary Quarterly*, III (October 1965), 550.

4. Shklar, p. 680. The next quotation is from the same work and page.

5. J. Lesley, "A slap on the snout of the republican swine," quoted in Ian Grimble, *The Harington Family* (London, 1957), pp. 13 - 14; Blitzer, *An Immortal Commonwealth*, pp. 3 - 4.

6. Grimble, p. 14.

7. Various accounts of James Harrington's life exist but they do not vary significantly in regard to fact. The following section makes some use of all of these, but the interpretations of them in this text may differ from those advanced by others. In particular the reader is referred to Oliver Lawson

Dick, ed., *Aubrey's Brief Lives* (Ann Arbor, Michigan; 1962), pp. 124 - 27; John Toland, "The Life of James Harrington," pp. xi - xxxvii; Anthony Wood, *Athenae Oxoniensis*, ed. P. Bliss (London, 1817), III, 1115 - 26; Grimble; and Blitzer, *An Immortal Commonwealth*, pp. 1 - 62.

8. Grimble, p. 14.

9. Toland, p. xi.

10. Grimble, pp. 197 - 98. The next quotation is from the same work, p. 207.

11. Wood, p. 1116. The next quotation is from the same work and page.

12. Toland, p. xiv.

13. Wood, p. 1119.

14. Toland, p. xvii. This anecdote and the rest of the quotations come from this and succeeding pages in Toland.

15. Toland, p. xxx. This is a particularly interesting account, attributed to Harrington himself, of the interrogation he underwent after his arrest by agents of Charles II. Harrington defended his writings by saying that he wrote to show Cromwell what the true form of a commonwealth was and that if the law had allowed him to be punished "Oliver had done it," so exercised was the lord protector at the implied criticism.

16. Perez Zagorin, *The Court and the Country*, (New York, 1970), pp. 74 - 118.

17. Sir William Pelham, "A letter to Sec'y Conwell, April 21, 1623," quoted in Blitzer, *An Immortal Commonwealth*, p. 13.

18. Peter Laslett, *The World We Have Lost* (New York, 1965), p. 37. Much of the foregoing summary is based upon Laslett's deductions.

19. Trevor-Roper, pp. 22 - 24. This short history of the financial problems of some of the Harringtons follows Trevor-Roper closely.

20. Laslett, p. 48.

21. Pocock, "Machiavelli, Harrington, and English Political Ideologies," p. 556.

22. "The Prerogative," *Works*, p. 232.

Chapter Three

1. H. Ferne, D. D., "A letter to Lady Ashton, November 4, 1656," quoted in "Pian Piano," *Works*, pp. 517 - 18.

2. "Oceana," *Works*, pp. 36 - 37; Liljegren, p. 14.

3. "Oceana," *Works*, p. 41; Liljegren, p. 20. The next quotation is from the same works, p. 42; p. 20.

4. "Oceana," *Works*, p. 42; Liljegren, p. 21. The next quotation is from the same works, p. 42; p. 21.

5. Matthew Wren, *Considerations on Mr. Harrington's Commonwealth of Oceana*, quoted in Blitzer, *An Immortal Commonwealth*, p. 39.

6. "Oceana," *Works*, p. 43; Liljegren, p. 22.

7. "Oceana," *Works*, p. 43; Liljegren, p. 22.

8. Richard Hooker, *Laws of Ecclesiastical Polity*, Book I, 3, 5, quoted in "Oceana," *Works*, p. 43; Liljegren, p. 22.

9. "Oceana," *Works*, p. 43; Liljegren, p. 22.

10. "Oceana," *Works*, p. 43; Liljegren, p. 22.

11. "Oceana," *Works*, p. 44; Liljegren, p. 23. The next two quotations are from the same work, p. 44; p. 23; and p. 45; p. 25.

12. Hobbes, *Leviathan*, p. 214. As quoted in "Oceana," *Works*, p. 49; Liljegren, pp. 24 - 30. The next several paragraphs are a summary of the argument in *Oceana* on this point.

13. "Oceana," *Works*, p. 50; Liljegren, pp. 31 - 32.

14. "Oceana," *Works*, p. 51; Liljegren, p. 32.

15. "Oceana," *Works*, p. 51; Liljegren, p. 32. The next two quotations are from the same work, p. 51; p. 32.

16. "Oceana," *Works*, p. 51; Liljegren, p. 33.

17. "Oceana," *Works*, p. 53; Liljegren, pp. 34 - 35.

18. "Oceana," *Works*, pp. 55 - 56; Liljegren, p. 38.

19. Michael Oakeshott, "Rationalism in Politics," *Cambridge Journal*, I (1947), p. 96.

20. "Oceana," *Works*, p. 112; Liljegren, p. 102.

21. "Oceana," *Works*, p. 121; Liljegren, p. 114.

22. Wren, quoted in "The Prerogative," *Works*, p. 226.

23. Wren, quoted in "The Prerogative," *Works*, pp. 234 - 35. The next two quotations are from the same work, pp. 235 - 36, and p. 238.

24. Wren, quoted in "The Prerogative," *Works*, p. 242.

25. "The Prerogative," *Works*, p. 248.

26. "The Prerogative," *Works*, p. 291. The next three paragraphs contain a summary of the remainder of *The Prerogative*.

27. Both pamphlets are contained in *Works*, pp. 508 - 15, and pp. 491 - 505. The summaries that follow are based on these texts.

28. "Seven Models of a Commonwealth," *Works*, p. 491.

29. Both pamphlets are contained in Harrington, *Works*, pp. 562 - 66 and pp. 567 - 74. Summaries of both follow.

30. Harrington, "A Discourse upon this saying. . . ," *Works*, p. 568.

31. This work is contained in *Works*, pp. 359 - 438.

32. "The Art of Lawgiving," *Works*, p. 403.

33. "The Art of Lawgiving," *Works*, p. 436. The next quotation is taken from the same work, p. 437.

34. "A Discourse upon this saying. . . ," *Works*, pp. 574.

35. "Seven Models," *Works*, p. 498.

36. The description of the influence of Venice and its historians upon European and English political theorists contained in this section is based upon Z. S. Fink, *The Classical Republicans* (Evanston, 1962), pp. 28 - 122.

37. Marchamont Needham, *The Excellency of a Free State*, quoted in G. P. Gooch, *English Democratic Ideas in the 17th Century* (New York, 1959), p. 243.

38. J. W. Gough, "Harrington and Contemporary Thought," *Political Science Quarterly*, XLV (1930), 395 - 404. Gough, of all who have written on this aspect of Harrington's thought, is alone in holding this opinion.

39. Dick, pp. 63 - 64.

Chapter Four

1. Dick, p. xvii. The next quotation is from Aubrey's diary quoted in Dick, p. xviii.

2. "Oceana," *Works*, p. 170; Liljegren, p. 175.

3. Thomas Herbert, *Memoirs*, p. 65, quoted in Gooch, p. 252. The next quotation is from the same work and page.

4. "The Prerogative," *Works*, p. 224. The next quotation is from the same work and page.

5. "Oceana," *Works*, p. 58; Liljegren, p. 41. The following account of Harrington's history of Europe is based upon "Preliminaries II" in *Oceana*.

6. "Oceana," *Works*, p. 62; Liljegren, p. 46.

7. "Oceana," *Works*, p. 63; Liljegren, p. 47.

8. "Oceana," *Works*, p. 64; Liljegren, p. 48.

9. "Oceana," *Works*, p. 65; Liljegren, p. 49.

10. "Oceana," *Works*, p. 66; Liljegren, p. 51. The next quotation is from the same work, p. 67; p. 53.

11. C. B. MacPherson, "Harrington: The Opportunity State," in *The Political Theory of Possessive Individualism* (Oxford, 1964), p. 162.

12. "The Prerogative," *Works*, p. 229.

13. "A System of Politics," *Works*, p. 471. Harrington makes the same point, though not so well, in other works.

14. "The Prerogative," *Works*, p. 279. The next quotation is from the same work and page.

15. Pocock, *The Ancient Constitution*, p. 129. The previous quotation is from the same work and page.

16. Laslett, pp. 156 - 57; the description of the "putting out" system that follows is based upon Laslett, p. 16.

17. This criticism of Seldon and Harrington is fully developed in Pocock, *The Ancient Constitution*, pp. 137 - 42.

18. Dick, p. xxxiv.

19. "The Art of Lawgiving," *Works*, p. 403.

20. "Political Aphorisms," *Works*, p. 488.

21. Blitzer, *An Immortal Commonwealth*, pp. 96 - 99.

22. "Political Aphorisms," *Works*, p. 488.

23. "The Prerogative," *Works*, p. 232.

24. "Valerius and Publicola," *Works*, p. 461. "That what neither is, nor ever was in nature, can never be in nature."

25. Blitzer, *An Immortal Commonwealth*, pp. 94 - 95.

26. "A System of Politics," *Works*, p. 468.

27. "The Prerogative," *Works*, p. 215.

Chapter Five

1. Both of these samples of satire at Harrington's expense appear in H. F. Russell-Smith, *Harrington and His Oceana* (Cambridge, 1914), pp. 99 - 101.

2. The following summary of *Oceana* follows the text closely.

3. "Oceana," *Works*, p. 100; Liljegren, p. 94.

4. "Oceana," *Works*, p. 102; Liljegren, p. 97.

5. Blitzer, *An Immortal Commonwealth*, p. 257.

6. "Oceana," *Works*, p. 168; Liljegren, p. 173.

7. "Oceana," *Works*, p. 174; Liljegren, p. 180.

8. "Oceana," *Works*, p. 210; Liljegren, p. 225.

9. Both pamphlets are contained in Harrington, *Works*, pp. 542 - 45 and pp. 584 - 85.

10. This pamphlet is contained in *Works*, pp. 580 - 83.

11. The text of this petition, under the title "The humble Petition of divers well-affected Persons," is contained in *Works*, pp. 508 - 13.

12. Among many who attended are Henry Nevill, Maximilian Petty (related to, and associated with, Oliver Cromwell), Sir John Hosbyus (later a president of the royal society), John Wildman (a noted radical), William Poultney, Roger Coke (author of *Detection of the four last Reigns*), and Major Venner.

13. Dick, p. 125. The next quotation is taken from the same work and page.

14. Samuel Pepys, *Diary*, quoted in Russell-Smith, p. 108.

15. Dick, p. 125.

16. Both pamphlets are contained in *Works*, pp. 506 - 507 and pp. 587 - 98.

17. "A Word Concerning a House of Peers," *Works*, p. 439. The next quotation is taken from the same work, p. 440.

18. An account of this examination is contained in Toland, pp. xxviii - xxxi.

19. Dick, p. 126.

20. This pamphlet, described as "imperfect" is contained in *Works*, pp. xxxviii - xi.

21. Toland, p. xxxiv.

22. "The Art of Lawgiving," *Works*, p. 403.

23. Pocock, "Machiavelli, Harrington, and English Political Ideologies," pp. 550 - 65. This section contains an excellent description of this group and serves as the basis for this summary of their position and ideology.

24. Russell-Smith, p. 152.

25. Ibid., pp. 167 - 79.

26. Ibid., pp. 187 - 97.

27. Ibid., pp. 201 - 209.

Selected Bibliography

PRIMARY SOURCES

All of the political works, books, and pamphlets of James Harrington were published in London during the period 1656 - 1660 except for two that were written later and published after his death. Two translations of Virgil by Harrington were published in 1659. A collection of all but one of the political works was made by John Toland who published a volume containing what he thought were the ten most important of these in 1700. These ten, together with an appendix containing eleven more works, were published in 1737, 1747, and 1771 in London. Two editions were published in Dublin in 1737 and 1758. These various Toland editions plus the Liljegren edition of *Oceana* and some selections edited by Charles Blitzer are the scholar's major Harrington sources.

The Commonwealth of Oceana. Ed., Sven B. Liljegren. Heidelberg: Carl Winters, 1924. This edition is easy to read and Liljegren's notes are extensive and helpful.

Works: The Oceana and Other Works. Ed., John Toland. 1771 ed.; rpt. Darmstadt: Scientia Verlag Aalen, 1963.

The Political Writings of James Harrington. Ed., Charles Blitzer. New York: The Liberal Arts Press, 1955. Selections are from *A System of Politics, The Commonwealth of Oceana,* and *The Rota.* Valuable introduction by the editor.

SECONDARY SOURCES

1. Books

ALLEN, J. W. *A History of Political Thought in the Sixteenth Century.* New York: Barnes and Noble, 1960. Survey of the political theory that immediately preceded the era in which Harrington wrote.

BLITZER, CHARLES. *An Immortal Commonwealth.* New Haven: Yale University Press, 1960. Most extensive study given Harrington as a man and theorist. This book and Liljegren's edition of *Oceana* are indispensable to Harrington scholars.

DICK, OLIVER LAWSON, ed. *Aubrey's Brief Lives.* Ann Arbor: University of Michigan Press, 1962. Amusing short biographies of Harrington and his contemporaries by a man who knew everyone.

FILMER, ROBERT. *Patriarcha and Other Political Works.* Ed., Peter Laslett. Oxford: Basil Blackwell, 1949. Writings of an interesting Royalist publicist provide an interesting contrast to Harrington.

FINK, Z. S. *The Classical Republicans.* Evanston, Ill. Northwestern University Press, 1962. Traces republican thought in seventeenth century England to its origins. Especially good in examining the influence of Venice on this current of political thought.

FIRTH, C. H. *The Last Years of the Protectorate.* 2 vols. New York: Russell and Russell, 1964. Almost day-by-day account of the period.

GOOCH, G. P. *English Democratic Ideas in the 17th Century.* New York: Harper and Brothers, 1959. Places Harrington in the tradition of Western democracy.

GRIMBLE, IAN. *The Harington Family.* London: n.p., 1957. Excellent history of Harrington's family and its contribution to English political life and culture.

JUDSON, MARGARET. *The Political Thought of Henry Vane the Younger.* Philadelphia: University of Pennsylvania Press, 1969. Vane, a contemporary of Harrington's, sympathized with but differed from his views.

LASLETT, PETER. *The World We Have Lost.* New York: Charles Scribner's Sons, 1965. Social history of England in the seventeenth century; is consistently interesting about a period of history that has been written to death.

PETEGORSKY, DAVID W. *Left Wing Democracy in the English Civil War.* London: Victor Gollancy Ltd., 1940. Marxist interpretation of the civil war and its causes.

POCOCK, J. G. A. *The Ancient Constitution and the Feudal Law.* New York: W. W. Norton, 1967. Harrington's links with medieval law and custom are examined. A valuable study because this aspect of Harrington's theories has been ignored by most other commentators.

RAAB, FELIX. *The English Face of Machiavelli.* London: Routledge and Kegan Paul, 1964. First-rate examination of the influence of Machiavelli in England.

ROBBINS, CAROLINE. *The Eighteenth Century Commonwealthsmen.* Cambridge, Mass.: Harvard University Press, 1959. Contains an important examination of Whig political thought in the period after Harrington.

RUSSELL-SMITH, H. F. *Harrington and His Oceana: A Study of a 17th Century Utopia and Its Influence in America.* Cambridge: Cambridge University Press, 1914. The best treatment of Harrington's influence.

TAWNEY, R. H. *Harrington's Interpretation of His Age.* London: Humphrey Milford, 1941. Important work in the developing controversy over Harrington and the "Rise of the Gentry."

TREVELYAN, GEORGE. *England Under the Stuarts.* London: Methueu and Co., 1949. Standard history of the period.

TREVOR-ROPER, H. R. *The Gentry 1540 - 1640.* London: Cambridge University Press, n.d. Harrington is firmly placed in the ranks of the declining gentry.

ZAGORIN, PEREZ. *The Court and the Country.* New York: Atheneum, 1970.

Lucid treatment of the major political factions in the English Civil War.

————. *A History of Political Thought in the English Revolution.* London: Routledge and Kegan Paul, 1954. Important for an understanding of the splendid flowering of political thought at the time and the personal and intellectual relationships of the thinkers and writers.

WOOD, ANTHONY. *Athenae Oxoniensis.* Ed., P. Bliss. London: n.p., 1817. Short, intellectual biographies of Harrington and his contemporaries.

2. Articles

BLUHM, WILLIAM T. "Naturalistic Political Science as Interest Group Theory: Harrington and Bentley." In *Theories of the Political System*, pp. 330 - 58. Englewood Cliffs: Prentice-Hall, Inc., 1964. Links Harrington with modern political science.

DWIGHT, THEODORE. "James Harrington and His Influence upon American Political Institution and Political Thought." *Political Science Quarterly*, II (1887), 1ff. An earlier treatment of the subject treated by Russell-Smith.

GOUGH, J. W. "Harrington and Contemporary Thought." *Political Science Quarterly*, XLV (1930), 395 - 404.

HEXTER, J. H. "Storm Over the Gentry." *Encounter*, (May 1958), pp. 22 - 34. A level-headed examination of the "Rise of the Gentry" controversy.

HILL, CHRISTOPHER. "The English Civil War Interpreted by Marx and Engles." *Science and Society, a Marxian Quarterly*, XII (1948), 130 - 56. The class struggle in seventeenth century England.

LEVETT, A. E. "James Harrington." In *Social and Political Ideas of the Sixteenth and Seventeenth Centuries.* Ed., F. J. C. Hearnshaw, pp. 174 - 202. New York: Barnes and Noble, 1949. Generally unsympathetic portrait of Harrington.

MACPHERSON, C. B. "Harrington: The Opportunity State." In *The Political Theory of Possessive Individualism*, pp. 160 - 93. London: Oxford University Press, 1962. Harrington effectively presented as a bourgeois political theorist.

POCOCK, J. G. A. "Machiavelli, Harrington, and English Political Ideologies in the Eighteenth Century." *William and Mary Quarterly*, III (1965), 549 - 83. Excellent treatment of the neo-Harringtonians.

SHKLAR, JUDITH N. "Ideology Hunting: The Case of James Harrington." *American Political Science Review*, LIII (1959), 662 - 92. A very good place to start any study of James Harrington. Professor Shklar offers so many leads and makes such important basic distinctions that her article is an indispensable aid in establishing scholarly perspective.

TAWNEY, R. H. "The Rise of the Gentry, 1558 - 1640." *The Economic History Review*, XI (1941), 1 - 38. The case identifying Harrington with a rising gentry.

Index

DATE DUE
